Read Me First!

About Fig Leaf Software

Fig Leaf Software is an award-winning team of imaginative designers, innovative developers, approachable instructors, and insightful strategists.

For over 20 years, we've helped a diverse range of clients with needs across the entire spectrum of web-related services, including design, marketing and content strategies, custom software development, product licensing and personalized training.

Located in the heart of Washington, DC, we're a Certified Service-Disabled Veteran-Owned Small Business (SD-VOSB) with a keen ability to understand your needs, a broad array of strategic Partners, and a talented team eager to make your latest web initiative a resounding success.

Fig Leaf maintains close partnerships with Acquia, Adobe, Amazon, Google, Sencha, HubSpot, Salesforce.com, and other thought-leaders in web application development and web content management.

Check us out at http://www.figleaf.com and http://training.figleaf.com.

Whether you need strategic consulting, best practice guidance, or products and training for real-world solutions, *We've Got You Covered.*

About Leo Schuman

Leo has been coding, writing, recording, and delivering technical training for software developers since 1997. He's taught languages, frameworks, content management, and persistence systems for Couchbase, Datastax, Fig Leaf, Adobe, Macromedia, and Allaire. And, he's lived in Portland, Oregon, since Bud Clark exposed himself to art.

Configuring your Workstation

Please see appendix A on page 261 for instructions on how to configure your workstation. You can download the course exercise files from the following url:

http://www.github.com/sdruckerfig/ftjq

Register your Book!

Go online and register your book to receive free content updates and news alerts!

http://go.figleaf.com/book

Get Trained by a Certified Instructor

Feeling a little overwhelmed by the volume of material contained in this book? Try taking one of our instructor-led courses which are offered either in-person or online:

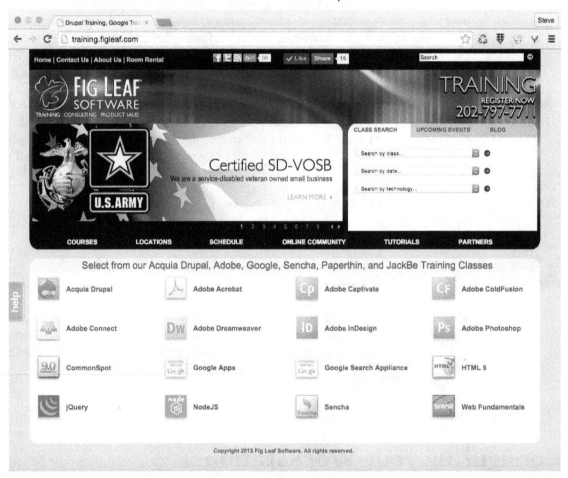

http://training.figleaf.com/

Table of Contents

Unit 0
Introducing the course

About the course

Fast Track to jQuery is designed for experienced web developers, and code-savvy web designers, seeking a thorough hands-on training in the jQuery JavaScript framework, and related jQuery plugins.

This 3 day course is task-based, involving numerous detailed instructor led programming exercises, accompanied by lab scenarios challenging you to remember what you have learned, and put your skills to work with limited guidance and supervision.

Objectives

After completing this course, you should be able to:

- Understand jQuery in relation to JavaScript and other frameworks

- Deploy jQuery and use common JavaScript debugging and development tools

- Understand jQuery framework terminology and the page query paradigm

- Precisely select and iterate page elements and element sets

- Modify element content and attributes explicitly or dynamically

- Request and load remote content by page or element

- Request, parse, and use remote JSON and XML data

- Add, move, remove, clone, create, and replace page elements

- Dynamically modify CSS styles

- Understand, implement, and control jQuery and custom event handlers

- Implement jQuery UI interactions, widgets, and effects

- Implement jQuery form input validation

Prerequisites

We assume students who have registered for this course:

- Understand HTML and can code HTML by hand in a text editor
- Understand basic CSS and can code basic CSS by hand in a text editor
- Have experience programming with variables, loops, conditions, and functions
- Have exposure to event-driven programming
- Have exposure to working with XML and JSON data formats

Course Format

Concepts introduce new information through explanations and code samples

Demonstrations provide visually guided explanations by the instructor

Exercises provide you hands-on coding experience guided by the instructor

Labs challenge you to use what you have learned with minimal guidance

Summaries provide a brief synopsis of the content you have completed

Reviews challenge you to remember what you learned in a prior unit

Course Outline

1. Introducing the Course
2. Reviewing core JavaScript concepts and best practices
   a. Organizing and accessing your files
   b. Reviewing JavaScript fundamentals
3. Introducing jQuery
   a. Comparing jQuery and the alternatives
   b. Deploying jQuery
   c. Introducing core terminology
   d. Surveying jQuery Fundamentals
4. Traversing elements with selectors
   a. Introducing the page query paradigm
   b. Selecting page elements
   c. Adding precision to page queries
   d. Accessing selected elements

References

jQuery Documentation

http://docs.jquery.com/

jQuery Source Code

http://docs.jquery.com/Source_Code

jQuery Forum

http://forum.jquery.com/

jQuery Toolchain Options

http://stackoverflow.com/questions/1480186/what-is-in-your-javascript-toolchain

Unit I
Reviewing JavaScript and best practices

Objectives

After completing this module, you should understand the fundamentals of:

- Organizing your files and tools
- Using simple and complex variables, loops, and conditions
- Accessing page elements by ID
- Implementing event listeners and handlers
- Using functions, anonymous functions, scope, and closures

Organizing your files and finding your tools

Reviewing HTML and JavaScript file structure

Adding JavaScript to a page

JavaScript may be defined three ways: inline with HTML, in page level *<script>* blocks, or in external files. The *<script>* block may appear any number of times, anywhere in either the *<head>* or *<body>* of the page. Script may also be loaded from an external file.

```
<!-- inline JavaScript -->
<button onclick="sayHello('world');">Say Hello (inline)</button>


<!-- page level JavaScript -->
<script>
      function sayHello2(name) {
            alert('Hello ' + name + '!');
      }
</script>
<button onclick="sayHello2('world');">Say Hello (page)</button>


<!-- external JavaScript -->
<button id="world">Say Hello (external)</button>
<script src="js/script.js"></script>
```

The best practice is to load all scripts from external files.

Understanding how the browser loads JavaScript

While browsers load other page elements in parallel, *<script>* elements load synchronously, blocking all other elements from loading until complete. As a result, it is common practice to load *<script>* elements at the bottom of a page, after the page elements are loaded.

```
        ...
        <script src="js/script.js"></script>
</body>
</html>
```

Organizing files on the file system

It is common to store all CSS and JavaScript in relevantly named sub-folders of the folder from which HTML pages will be requested.

Finding and choosing your development tools

Choosing a text editor

Because HTML, JavaScript, and CSS are not compiled, any text editor may be used for development. That being said, additional developer features such as highlighting, lookup, and tag completion can save valuable time. Some choices include:

Sublime Text 2
http://www.sublimetext.com/2

Jetbrains WebStorm
http://www.jetbrains.com/webstorm/

Notepad++
http://notepad-plus-plus.org/

TextMate
http://macromates.com/

Reviewing the commonly available tools

Name and location vary by browser, but major browsers support informational displays of:

Console: displays debugging information written from JavaScript via *console.log, etc.*

Elements: enables selection, highlight, and attribute display of each page element

Resources: display off-page resources including cookies and other client-side data

Network: display XHR and similar data transfers

Source: display source of all page, script, and style files involved in the current page

Finding the JavaScript console and developer tools

All major browsers supports tools for examining page content and network traffic. Various tools will be used and explained in context during the course.

Chrome:
Tools > JavaScript Console
Tools > Developer Tools

Firefox:
Tools > Web Developer > Web Console
Tools > Web Developer > Firebug (additional plugin)

Safari: (Preferences > Advanced > Show Develop menu in menu bar)
Develop > Show Error Console

Internet Explorer 9:
F12 > Console

Using console.log()

An *expression* is one or more *variables, functions,* or *operators* which can be evaluated together to produce a value. An expression passed to the built in *console.log()* method will be evaluated, and its result printed to the browser log.

```
var foo = 1;
var bar = 2;
console.log(foo + bar); // 3 is logged to the Javascript console
```

Reviewing JavaScript fundamentals

Reviewing basic syntax

Declaring a variable

JavaScript identifiers - variable and object names - are case-sensitive, and may be comprised of virtually any letters, characters, or numbers, but must begin with a letter, or the $ or _ .

```
name          // valid                name1        // valid
Name          // valid, and different first-name   // valid
$name         // valid                first_name   // valid
_name         // valid                firstName    // valid
1name         // not valid            7name        // not valid
```

The assignment (=) operator is used with an identifier declared using the *var* keyword.

```
var name = 'fred';
var size = 12;
var names = ['fred', 'ginger', 'sue'];
var person = {name:'fred', size:12};
```

Reserved words in JavaScript

The following words are either implemented as keywords, or reserved for future implementation in the language. They cannot be used as variable identifiers.

abstract	else	instanceof	super
boolean	enum	int	switch
break	export	interface	synchronized
byte	extends	let	this
case	FALSE	long	throw
catch	final	native	throws
char	finally	new	transient
class	float	null	TRUE
const	for	package	try
continue	function	private	typeof
debugger	goto	protected	var
default	if	public	void
delete	implements	return	volatile
do	import	short	while
double	in	static	with

In addition, avoid re-using the standard names of DOM objects, methods, properties, and events, as custom identifier names, as this may give unexpected results.

Understanding whitespace, tabs, and parentheses

Tabs and other whitespace have no meaning outside of quotations

```
var name =         'fred';      // no space around name
var name = '        fred';      // whitespace before name
```

Forcing operator precedence with parentheses

The default order of operations can be modified.

```
var result = 2 * 3 + 5          // result is 11
var result = 2 * ( 3 + 5 )      // result is 16
```

Enhancing readability with tabs

Tabbed code is more readable, but tabs have no effect on JavaScript execution.

```
var addNums = function( num1, num2 ) {
      return num1 + num2;
};
```

Reviewing variables, math, and string operations

Concatenating strings

```
var greeting = 'Hello ';
var salutation = 'Mr.';
var firstName = 'Fred';
var lastName = 'Smith';

var fullName = firstName + ' ' + lastName;
// fullName is "Fred Smith"

var salutation + ' ' + fullName;
var greeting += salutation;
// greeting is "Hello Mr. Fred Smith"
```

Performing basic arithmetic

```
var result = 2 + 3;
// result is 5

var result = 2 - 3;
// result is -1

var result = 2 * 3;
// result is 6

var result = 2 / 3;
// result is .66666666666667
```

Incrementing and decrementing

```
var i = 1;

var j = ++i;
// pre-increment operator
// i becomes 2 then j becomes 2

var k = i++;
// post-increment operator
// k becomes 2 then i becomes 3
```

Comparing addition and concatenation

```
var foo = 1;
var bar = '2';

console.log( foo + bar );
// bar is a string, so console displays "12"

console.log( foo + Number(bar) );
// bar is coercible to a number, so console displays 3
```

Passing a string value to the *Number( )* constructor as a function, as above, converts the strings to its numeric value, if possible, else returns *NaN* (not a number).

Reviewing logical and comparison operators

Understanding true and false evaluation

Javascript evaluates these as true ("truthy")

```
'0'
'any string'
[ ]             // an empty array
{}              // an empty object
1               // any non-zero number, positive or negative
```

JavaScript evaluates these as false ("falsy")

```
0
' '             // an empty string
NaN             // Javascript's 'not a number' variable
null
undefined       // be careful — undefined can be redefined!
```

Using logical AND and OR operators

The logical operator && tests whether *both* of its operands evaluate as true. The && operator returns the value of the first "falsy" operand. Or, if both are truthy, it returns the last operand of the operation.

The logical operator || tests whether *either* of its operands evaluate as true. The || operator returns the value of the first "truthy" operand. Or, if neither is truthy, it returns the last operand of the operation.

```
var foo = 1, bar = 0, baz = 2;

foo || bar;    // returns 1, which is true
bar || foo;    // returns 1, which is true

foo && bar;    // returns 0, which is false
foo && baz;    // returns 2, which is true
baz && foo;    // returns 1, which is true
```

Using logical operators for flow control

Developers may use logical operators for flow control. While this creates elegantly terse code, it can be hard to follow, resulting in code which may be more difficult to maintain over time.

```
// do something with foo if foo is truthy
foo && doSomething( foo );

// set bar to baz if baz is truthy;
// otherwise, set it to the return
// value of createBar()
var bar = baz || createBar();
```

Reviewing comparison operators

Comparison operators test for either equivalency or identicality, which may not be the same.

```
var foo = 1, bar = 0, baz = '1', bim = 2;

foo == bar;    // returns false
foo != bar;    // returns true
foo == baz;    // returns true; careful!

foo === baz;              // returns false
foo !== baz;              // returns true
foo === parseInt(baz);    // returns true

foo > bim;     // returns false
bim > baz;     // returns true
foo <= baz;    // returns true
```

Reviewing conditional code

Using conditional flow control statements

While comparison operations - which return *true* or *false* when evaluated - are often used in conditional flow control statements, remember that certain values are also treated as "truthy" (e.g., any non-zero number) or "falsy" (e.g., *NaN*).

```
var foo = true;
var bar = false;

if ( bar ) {
    // this code will never run
}

if ( bar ) {
    // this code won't run
} else {
    if ( foo ) {
        // this code will run
    } else {
        // this code would run if foo and bar were both false
    }
}
```

Single line conditions do not *require* a code block ({ ... }) but may be hard to read.

```
if ( status === 'Admin' ) return true;
```

Do not define functions which have the same name in different conditional blocks, as both may be read by the parser - despite the conditions - with one overriding the other.

Conditionally assigning variables

The ternary operator enables variable assignment based on a condition. If the first value is true, then second value is assigned, else the third value is assigned.

```
// set foo to 1 if bar is true;
// otherwise, set foo to 0
var foo = bar ? 1 : 0;
```

Testing the same expression for multiple values

The *switch* statement tests one variable or expression against multiple cases, executing the first matching case, and all subsequent cases, unless a *break* statement is used. An optional *default* case may be assigned.

```
switch ( foo ) {
    case 'bar':
        alert( 'the value was bar -- yay!' );
    break;

    case 'baz':
        alert( 'boo baz :(' );
    break;

    default:
        alert( 'everything else is just ok' );
    break;
}
```

Using dynamic method calls on an object, in place of a switch

A more flexible alternative to switch statements, often used in modern JavaScript, is to define an object with functions assigned as the values of its properties, then dynamically reference these properties ("methods") using the variable or expression to be evaluated.

```
var stuffToDo = {
    'bar' : function() {
        alert( 'the value was bar -- yay!' );
    },

    'baz' : function() {
        alert( 'boo baz :(' );
    },

    'default' : function() {
        alert( 'everything else is just ok' );
    }
};
```

Note, it is "truthy" for a dynamically referenced property to return a function, as here.

```
var foo = 'bar';
if ( stuffToDo[foo] ) {
    stuffToDo[foo]();
} else {
    stuffToDo['default']();
}
```

Objects and dynamic property referencing are discussed further ahead.

Reviewing iteration ("looping") statements

JavaScript supports four basic loop types, each of which may be nested in any other, as needed, to iterate across multiple dimensions.

- *for*
- *for-in*
- *while*
- *do-while*

Using the for loop

The *for* loop initializes, tests, and changes its own iteration variable. Multiple values may be initialized, tested, and incremented or decrement.

```
for ( var i = 0, limit = 100; i < limit; i++ ) {
        // This block will be executed 100 times
        console.log( 'Currently at ' + i );

        // The first log will be "Currently at 0"
        // The last log will be "Currently at 99"
}
```

Using the for-in loop

The *for-in* loop iterates the properties of an object, exposing each property name in turn through its iteration variable.

```
var person = { name:'Ginger', age:36, admin:true };
for ( var propertyName in person ) {
        console.log( propertyName + ':' + person[propertyName] );

        // The console will display
        // name:Ginger
        // age:36
        // admin:true
}
```

Objects, arrays, and dynamic property referencing are discussed in more detail further ahead.

Using the while loop

A *while* loop will execute indefinitely until its condition returns *false*. Its iteration variable must be explicitly created and incremented.

```
var i = 0;
while ( i < 100 ) {

        // This block will be executed 100 times
        console.log( 'Currently at ' + i );

        // increment the tested variable, else run forever
        i++;
}
```

Using the do-while loop

The *do-while* loop varies from a while loop, in that it will always execute at least one time, whereas a while loop may never execute if its condition is initially false.

```
var i = 100;
do {
        // This block will execute only once
        console.log( 'Currently at ' + i );

        // you must still change the tested variable, else run forever
        i++;

} while ( i < 100 )
```

Breaking out of a loop

You may wish to end the loop if a nested condition is *true*. The *break* keyword ends a loop, and execution continues immediately after the loop block.

```
var names = ['Fred', 'Ginger', 'Jane', 'Sue'];
for ( var i = 0; i < names.length; i++ ) {
        if ( names[i] === 'Jane' ) {
                // loop ends once "Jane" is found
                break;
        }
}
console.log( names[i] + ' was found' );
// The console will display "Jane was found"
```

Continuing to the next iteration of a loop

You may wish to skip processing the rest of a loop block if a nested condition is *false*. The *continue* keyword ends the current iteration of a loop, and starts the next.

```
var names = ['Fred', 'Ginger', 'Jane', 'Sue'];
for ( var i = 0; i < names.length; i++ ) {
        if ( names[i] !== 'Jane' ) {
                // loop restarts unless "Jane" is found
                continue;
        }
        console.log( names[i] + ' was found' );
}
// The console will display "Jane was found"
```

Reviewing complex variables

A complex variable is one which holds an indefinite number of values. JavaScript provides two complex variable types, the *array* and the *object*.

An *array* holds or refers to an indefinite number of distinct values or objects, identified by *numbers* beginning with 0, known as *indices* of that array.

```
var names = [ 'Fred', 'Ginger' ];
console.log( names[1] );
// log displays "Ginger"
```

An *object* holds or refers to an indefinite number of distinct values or objects, identified by *words* known as *properties* or *member variables* of that object.

```
var person = { name:'Fred', age:42 };
console.log( person.name );
// log displays "Fred"
```

Creating and populating arrays

Arrays are *heterogeneous*: each value may be a distinct type (string, number, object reference, etc.). They are also *dynamic*: they may grow or shrink to hold any number of values.

The following statements created and populate an identical array.

```
var a1 = [ 'Fred', 12, 0x00ff00 ];
var a2 = new Array( 'Fred', 12, 0x00ff00 );
var a3 = new Array();
a3.push( 'Fred' );
a3.push( 12 );
a3.push( 0x00ff00 );
```

Accessing an array's values

In basic JavaScript, arrays are often accessed using loops. The *.length* property identifies the number of values in the array. The *.pop()* method removes and returns the highest-index value.

```
var names = [ 'Fred', 'Ginger' ];
for ( var i = 0; i < names.length; i++ ) {
        console.log( names[i] );
        // console displays values first to last, and remains populated
        // "Fred"
        // "Ginger"
}
console.log( names ); // displays "['Fred', 'Ginger']"

while ( names.length > 0 ) {
        console.log( names.pop() );
        // console displays values, and is de-populated
        // "Ginger"
        // "Fred
}
console.log( names ); // displays "[]"
```

Creating and populating an object

Objects are variables to which other variables as well as functions may be attached as *members*. *Member variables* may also be called *properties*. *Member functions* may also be called *methods*.

Objects may be created literally *inline*. Such objects may be referred to as *object literals*.

```
var person = {
        name:'Fred',
        age:42,
        getInfo : function() {
                return this.name + ':' + this.age;
        }
};
console.log( person.name ); // displays "Fred"
console.log( person.getInfo() ); // displays "Fred:42"
```

Objects may also be created by a *constructor function*.

```
function Person( name, age ) {
        this.name = name;
        this.age = age;
        this.getInfo = function() {
                return this.name + ':' + this.age;
        }
}
var person = new Person( 'Fred', 42 );
console.log( person.name ); // displays "Fred"
console.log( person.getInfo() ); // displays "Fred:42"
```

Unlike other object-oriented languages, JavaScript does not support *class* definitions. Functions and the *this* keyword will be discussed in more detail further ahead.

Accessing object properties dynamically

Object members - whether variables/properties or functions/methods - may be explicitly referenced using the *dot operator* (*person.name*) or dynamically referenced using *array notation* (*person["name"]*).

```
var person = { name:'Fred', age: 42 };
console.log( person.name );          // displays "Fred"
console.log( person['name'] );       // displays "Fred"
```

When using array notation, either a string literal or a variable containing or function returning a string literally may be used.

```
var person = { name:'Fred', age: 42 };
var propertyName = 'name';
var getName = function() { return 'name' };
console.log( person[propertyName] );   // displays "Fred"
console.log( person[getName()] );      // displays "Fred"
```

Iterating the properties of an object

The *for-in loop* discussed previously relies on dynamically referencing an object's members.

```
var person = { name:'Fred', age:42, getInfo :
     function() { return this.name + ':' + this.age; }
};

for( var member in person ) {
     console.log (member + ':' + person[member] );
}
// console displays:
// name:Fred
// age:42
// getInfo: function() { return this.name + ':' + this.age; }
```

Notice that the console displays the function, but does not *call* the function.

Reviewing functions, arguments, and references

Declaring a function and referencing its arguments

A *function* is a named block of code which may be called and executed by referring to its name followed by parentheses. The function may be passed *arguments* (also known as "parameters").

```
function addNums( num1, num2 ) {
     return num1 + num2;
}
console.log( addNums( 2, 3 ) );  // displays 5
```

If arguments are passed, they may be referenced by their name or through an automatically created *arguments array*.

```
function addNums( num1, num2 ) {
     console.log( arguments.length ); // displays 2
     return arguments[0] + arguments[1];
}
console.log( addNums( 2, 3 ) );  // displays 5
```

Assigning a function to a variable or property

A function may be explicitly named, or declared without a name (*anonymously*) and assigned to a variable. The following code declares the same function two different ways.

```
function addNums( num1, num2 ) { return num1 + num2; }

var addNums = function( num1, num2 ) { return num1 + num2 };
```

The variable to which an *anonymous function* is assigned may itself be a member of an object, in which case the *function* becomes a *method* of that object.

```
var person = {
        name:'Fred',
        age:42,
        getInfo : function() {
                return this.name + ':' + this.age;
        }
};
```

Using a function to declare another function

Functions are just another type of object. So they may be declared by another function and then assigned to one of its member variables, just like any other value.

```
function Person( name, age ) {
        this.name = name;
        this.age = age;
        this.getInfo = function() {
                return this.name + ':' + this.age;
        }
}
var person = new Person( 'Fred', 42 );
console.log( person.name ); // displays "Fred"
console.log( person.getInfo() ); // displays "Fred:42"
```

Reviewing self-executing functions

Functions written as expressions - surrounded by parentheses and followed by the arguments operator (more parentheses) - execute immediately when parsed by the browser, without being explicitly called.

```
(function foo() {
        // do something
})();
```

Understanding the keyword this inside an object

Generally speaking, the keyword *this* refers to the object through which the currently executing code has been called. So, when used in a function assigned to an object - in a *method* of that object - *this* refers to that object.

```
function Person( name, age ) {
      this.name = name;
      this.age = age;
      this.getInfo = function() {
            return this.name + ':' + this.age;
      }
}
var person1 = new Person( 'Fred', 42 );
console.log( person1.getInfo() ); // displays "Fred:42"
var person2 = new Person( 'Ginger', 37 );
console.log( person2.getInfo() ); // displays "Ginger:37"
```

Understanding the keyword: new

The *new* keyword creates a new object, and passes it as an anonymous argument to a function which is called immediately following the *new* keyword.

```
var person1 = new Person( 'Fred', 42 );
```

Inside the function, this new object is referenced using the *this* keyword. Variables may be assigned to *this*, thereby attaching them to this new object, which is automatically returned by the function - known as a *constructor function* - and may be assigned to another variable.

```
function Person( name, age ) {
      this.name = name;
      this.age = age;
      this.getInfo = function() {
            return this.name + ':' + this.age;
      }
}
var person1 = new Person( 'Fred', 42 );
console.log( person1.getInfo() ); // displays "Fred:42"
```

Using this outside an object

When used in a regular, named function, the keyword *this* generally refers to the *window* object of the browser's Document Object Model (DOM).

```
function logBrowserSize() {
      console.log( this.innerHeight + ',' + this.innerWidth );
}
logBrowserSize();
// displays current pixel width and height of the browser window
```

Note that the keyword *this* is implied automatically when referencing the window object.

```
function logBrowserSize() {
      // innerHeight references window, without this
      console.log( innerHeight + ',' + innerWidth );
}
logBrowserSize();
// still displays current pixel width and height of the browser window
```

Reviewing JavaScript event handling

Events are signals dispatched indicating the browser or user have done something. Thousands of events are dispatched - almost all ignored - during a standard browser session.

Listening for and handling events

In basic JavaScript, an *event listener* may be assigned to listen for specific events on a specific object. And, an *event handler* function may be assigned. The event handler will be called each time the specified event occurs.

```
<button id='mybutton'>Click Me</button>
    ...
mybutton.addEventListener( "click", clickHandler );

function clickHandler() {
    console.log( 'something happened' );
}
// console displays "somebody clicked me"
```

Notice the event handler function is assigned as a reference, not called. So, no parentheses are used when it is passed to *.addEventListener(event type, handler function)*.

Explicitly named event handlers, such as this one, may be helpful when multiple different events may usefully rely on the same, single event handler.

Using anonymous, inline event handlers

JavaScript allows inline object creation. Functions are just another type of object. So, functions may be declared inline where needed. This code is functionally identical to the previous code.

```
<button id='mybutton'>Click Me</button>
    ...
mybutton.addEventListener( "click", function() {
    console.log( 'something happened' );
});
```

The jQuery library makes extensive use of anonymous inline functions.

Using the event object and this keyword in event handlers

Event handlers are automatically passed an event object as an argument, with properties describing - amongst other things - the *.type* ("what happened") and *.target* ("who did it") of the event. In the handler, the keyword *this* refers to the object dispatching the event.

```
<button id='mybutton'>Click Me</button>
    ...
mybutton.addEventListener( "click", function(event) {
    console.log( event.target.id + ':' + event.type );
    this.disabled = true;
});
// console displays "mybutton:click"
// and, button becomes disabled
```

Reviewing DOM manipulation

Retrieving page elements by ID

JavaScript treats a loaded page as a nested tree of elements within the Document Object Model (DOM). Elements with an ID may be accessed using *document.getElementById([id])*, and their content changed using the accessed element's *.innerHTML* property.

```
<div id="productName">DefaultName</div>
      ...
document.getElementById("productName").innerHTML="Acme Hopscotch Chalk";
```

A core goal of jQuery is to make page access simple, powerful, and consistent across browsers.

Reviewing scope

The term scope refers to where you can access a variable once it has been declared. In general terms, JavaScript recognizes two scopes: *global* and *local*.

Declaring and referencing global variables

Variables declared without the keyword *var* are defined on the *window* object. They are *global:* accessible anywhere on the page. This is generally a bad idea, as it makes code hard to follow.

```
var sayHello = function() {
      foo = 'hello';        // no var used
      console.log( foo );
};
sayHello();               // logs "hello"
console.log( foo );       // logs "hello"
console.log( window.foo );// logs "hello"
```

Declaring and referencing local variables

Local variables are declared using the keyword *var* and, once declared, can be accessed in the same block. They cannot be referenced outside that block.

```
var sayHello = function() {
      var foo = 'hello';
      console.log( foo );
};
sayHello();        // logs "hello"
console.log( foo ); // logs "Uncaught ReferenceError: foo is not defined"
```

Referencing local variables in nested functions

Local variables are also be accessible in functions nested inside the declaring function. The declaring function defines the outer reach of a variable, because each nested function is internally passed a set of references to its parent function's variables.

```
var sayHello = function() {
      var foo = "hello";
      function sayHello2() {
            console.log( foo );
      }
      sayHello2();
};
sayHello();           // logs "hello"
```

Reviewing JavaScript closures

Understanding the core concept of closures

A JavaScript closure is function to which the variables of its surrounding context are bound by reference. Every JavaScript function forms a closure, which is why nested functions have access to variables declared outside their block.

```
var sayHello = function() {
      var foo = "hello";
      function sayHello2() {
            console.log( foo );
      }
      sayHello2();
};
sayHello();          // logs "hello"
```

Closures, in conjunction with self-executing functions, are useful in controlling variable namespace and privacy at runtime. Patterns often used internally by the jQuery libraries - such as the module pattern - rely on closures.

Closures may also be referred to generally as *anonymous functions* or *lambdas*. However, to be a *closure*, specifically, the function must retain access to variables that were in scope when and where it was declared, even if they have otherwise fallen out of scope.

More detailed discussions of anonymous functions, closures, and the module pattern:

http://helephant.com/2008/08/23/javascript-anonymous-functions/

http://javascriptweblog.wordpress.com/2010/10/25/understanding-javascript-closures/

http://javascriptweblog.wordpress.com/2010/04/22/the-module-pattern-in-a-nutshell/

http://www.adequatelygood.com/2010/3/JavaScript-Module-Pattern-In-Depth

Summary

In this unit you have learned:

- Best practice is to store all JavaScript in external files

- Variable type is evaluated only as needed, as when concatenating numbers and strings

- Conditions are tested using *if*, *switch*, and the ternary operator

- Object collections are iterated using four loop constructs: *for*, *for-in*, *do*, *do-while*

- Functions are objects which may be assigned, whether named or anonymous

- Events are signals dispatched due to system or user actions, for which listeners may be assigned to call corresponding handler functions

- Elements with an ID may be accessed and modified at runtime

- Variables are scoped to the block in which they are declared, and are accessible to functions declared in the same block because all JavaScript functions are closures

Review

1. Describe two ways to display each value in an array

2. When might you declare an anonymous function?

3. Describe a data structure to hold the name, price, and image URL for an indefinite number of items to be displayed in an online catalog

4. If you declare a variable in functionOne, can you access it in functionTwo?

5. Why would you assign an ID attribute to an element?

Lab: Reviewing core JavaScript techniques

In this exercise you will declare and manipulate data using events, practicing with the syntax reviewed or learned in this unit.

After completion, you should be able to:

- Create the files for a basic interactive page
- Declare an object array using an object constructor function
- Write an event handler
- Access and display each value in an object array
- Write both named and anonymous functions

Steps

Create the files for a basic interactive page

1. In your file explorer, open this folder:

    `/ftjq/1-lab`

2. Create folders for CSS and JavaScript files.

3. In appropriate locations, create an *index.html* page, a *style.css* page, and a *script.js* page.

4. Write code to make the CSS and JavaScript files available to the HTML page.

5. Create a *button* named *showProducts* and a *div* named *display*.

Create an object array

6. Declare a function named *Product* which receives *name* and *price* arguments, and returns an object populated with these two values in corresponding properties.

7. Declare an array *products* with two new *Product* objects having *name* and *price* values.

Create an event handler to display each item in the array

8. Write a function which runs when the *showProducts* button is clicked.

9. In the *click* event handler, write a loop which logs a single line of text in the console for each product, displaying its *name* and *price*.

10. Write a function which receives a single *Product* object as an argument, and displays its *name* and *price* in the *div* named *display*, as a single line of text.

11. Call this function in the loop created above to display each item in the *products* array.

12. Verify that when you browse the page and click the button, the *name* and *price* of each *Product* is displayed both in the log and on the page.

13. One possible solution to the lab can be reviewed here:

    `/ftqj/1-lab-solution`

Unit 2
Introducing jQuery

Objectives

After completing this unit, you should understand:

- Deploying jQuery for your project
- Describing the jQuery function, the objects it creates, and their methods
- The fundamentals of configuring a page to use jQuery for
  - Selecting and modifying page element text and styles
  - Assigning event handlers to page elements
  - Creating new page elements, configuring them, and adding them to the page
  - Loading and using external JSON data

Comparing jQuery and its alternatives

Introducing jQuery

Understanding what jQuery is

jQuery is a JavaScript library designed to across all major browsers to simplify

- traversing page elements
- handling events
- setting and animating visual properties
- loading and managing external data

Understanding what jQuery is __not__

jQuery is not

- a set of pre-built user interface widgets
- a set of complex user interface interactions
- a prescriptive development framework

jQuery UI - which provides widgets and interactions, built on jQuery - is discussed later in this course. MVC development frameworks are not taught in this introductory course, but references will be provided.

Finding information about jQuery

jQuery is an open source project of the jQuery Foundation

jQuery Foundation
http://jquery.org/

jQuery Documentation
http://api.jquery.com/

jQuery Blog
http://blog.jquery.com

jQuery vs. raw JavaScript

Comparing jQuery to equivalent raw JavaScript

"JavaScript is an assembly language ... the browser can execute it, but no human should really care what's there." - Erik Meijer

Adding a CSS style in jQuery (works in <u>all</u> major browsers)

```
$("#mybox").addClass("mystyle");
```

Adding a CSS style in Modern JavaScript (does <u>not</u> work in all browsers)

```
var container = document.querySelector("#mybox");
container.classList.add("mystyle");
```

jQuery vs. other similar JavaScript libraries

Surveying the alternatives

jQuery is the most popular (by far) of many libraries addressing similar problems:

- Prototype, MooTools, YUI, and many others ...

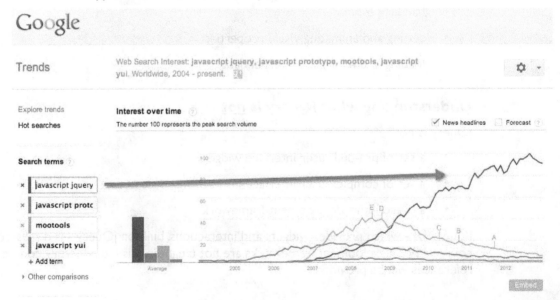

Deploying jQuery

Finding and downloading jQuery

Using jQuery in Development or Production versions

jQuery is deployed as a single large JavaScript file, in two versions:

http://jquery.com/download/

Development version
uncompressed code, for easy reading

Production version
minified and gzipped code, for fast transfer and parsing

Deploying jQuery

jQuery is commonly deployed from your own server scripts folder, like any JavaScript

1. select a jQuery version at jQuery.com

2. save the displayed JavaScript file to your JavaScript folder

3. link the script to your page like any other JavaScript file

```
    ...
    <script type="text/javascript" src="js/jquery-1.8.3.js"></script>
    <script type="text/javascript" src="js/script.js"></script>
</body>
</html>
```

Accessing jQuery using a Content Delivery Network (CDN)

Modern browsers cache script files. Major content delivery networks host jQuery. By linking to a CDN hosted copy, your page can rely on a cached version rather than load and parse its own.

Current links to CDN hosted jQuery versions are available at *http://jquery.com/download/*

*   Google Ajax Libraries API CDN
    https://ajax.googleapis.com/ajax/libs/jquery/1.9.0/jquery.min.js

*   Microsoft CDN
    http://ajax.aspnetcdn.com/ajax/jQuery/jquery-1.9.0.min.js

*   jQuery CDN, hosted by Media Temple
    http://code.jquery.com/jquery-1.9.0.min.js

Considerations in jQuery deployment and versioning

Running jQuery without conflicting with other versions or libraries

jQuery is accessed by default through the monolithic *jQuery(...)* function

```
jQuery("#myButton").click(function() { ... });
```

jQuery automatically exposes $ as a shorthand symbol for the *jQuery(...)* function

```
$("#myButton").ready(function() { ... });
```

Alternate symbols can be assigned to prevent conflict with other libraries or versions

```
var $jq = jQuery.noConflict();
$jq("#myButton").ready(function() { ... });
```

Introducing core jQuery terminology

Understanding jQuery in discussion

"<u>the</u> jQuery function"

jQuery(...) or *$(...)* itself, which provides access to the library as well as a single namespace for all of its functionality.

```
var allDivs = $("div");
// could also be: var allDivs = jQuery("div");
```

"a jQuery object"

The collection of zero or more page element references returned by the jQuery function when using it to select one or more page elements.

```
var allDivs = $("div");
```

"a jQuery function"

Static functions exposed by the jQuery function itself, such as *.noConflict()*.

```
$.each(allDivs, someFunction);
```

"a jQuery method"

The methods exposed by jQuery objects referencing specific page elements, which provide most of jQuery's power to manage and manipulate a page.

```
var allDivs = $("div");
allDivs.each(someFunction);
// commonly seen chained as: $("div").each(someFunction);
```

"element"

One specific DOM node selected using *the jQuery function* and returned for manipulation through the *jQuery methods* available when it is referenced as *a jQuery object*.

```
// functions are commonly passed anonymously to jQuery methods, as shown
$("div").each(function(index, element) {
        $(element).text("Foo" + index);
});
```

Surveying jQuery Fundamentals

To accelerate your learning, a core set of jQuery techniques will be introduced, followed by a detailed hands-on exercise. Each topic will be discussed in more detail throughout the course.

Accessing jQuery on the page

Controlling scope and the meaning of $

JQuery is commonly used with other libraries which:

- may also use the $ symbol

- may create other variable naming conflicts

As an alternative to re-naming using *jQuery.noConflict()*, scope and namespace can be controlled by executing all jQuery code within a closure created by a self-executing function.

```
(function($) {
// place *all* jQuery script in this block

})(jQuery);
```

Using $(document).ready

Ensuring page load before code execution

jQuery dispatches a ready event when the document is loaded and fully parsed. Code run prior to this risks accessing elements not yet available. Commonly, all jQuery code is written within the handler for this event.

```
(function($) {
    $(document).ready(function() {
    // place *all* jQuery script in this block

    });
})(jQuery);
```

Using an alternative syntax for the ready event

A more cryptic shorthand may be used in place of the standard $(document).ready syntax, due to jQuery's default treatment of a function passed to it as an argument.

```
(function($) {
    $(function() {
    // place *all* jQuery script in this block

    });
})(jQuery);
```

Selecting page elements with jQuery

Using selectors with the jQuery function

The core purpose of jQuery is to access page elements for manipulation and event handling. It supports a robust selection syntax to access corresponding elements, individually or as a set.

```
// select all div's assigned a CSS class named display, and assign text
$("div.display").text("foo");
```

```
// select the one element with ID mybutton and set its disabled property true
$("#mybutton").prop("disabled", "true");
```

Adding an event handler

Configuring jQuery objects to handle page element events

jQuery enables page element attributes and events to be handled using a single syntax, despite lingering browser variations. Handler functions may be written inline or separately.

In an event handler, *this* refers to the dispatching object, and can be used to create a jQuery object for manipulating the dispatcher.

```
// disable this button after it is clicked
$("#mybutton").click(function() {
        $(this).prop("disabled", "true");
});
```

```
// assign a separate handler function (e.g., one used by many elements)
$("#mybutton").click(clickHandler); // object reference, no parentheses
function clickHandler() {
        $(this).prop("disabled", "true");
}
```

Exercise: Surveying jQuery Fundamentals - **Part 1**

In this two-part exercise you will configure a page to create and display an element for each item in an externally loaded data collection.

After completion of Part 1, you should have a basic understanding of how to:

- Configure HTML pages to use jQuery without scope and shorthand conflicts

- Use jQuery to assign listeners and handle events

NOTE: This exercise quickly covers many techniques to provide an initial overview of using jQuery. All topics in this exercise are discussed in much further detail throughout the course.

Steps

Review and configure project files

1. Open the following project and review its starting HTML, CSS, and JSON files:

    `/ftjq/2-jq-fundamentals`

2. Browse the project's *index.html* file to verify your local web server is working:

    `http://localhost:8888/ftjq/2-jq-fundamentals/`

3. Download a development copy of jQuery to this folder:

    `/ftjq/2-jq-fundamentals/js`

4. Create a new file named *script.js* and save it to this folder:

    `/ftjq/2-jq-fundamentals/js`

5. Link the *jquery-[version].js* and *script.js* files to the bottom of *index.html*.

    ```
    ...
    <script type="text/javascript" src="js/jquery-1.8.3.js"></script>
    <script type="text/javascript" src="js/script.js"></script>
    </body>
    </html>
    ```

Configure script.js for jQuery and test .ready event

6. In *js/script.js*, add a self-executing function which receives the jQuery object as an argument named *$*.

7. In the scope block, add a jQuery document *ready* event handler, using the shorthand *$* reference to the jQuery object.

8. In the document *ready* event handler, open an *alert* box to test the event handler.

9. Your code should look like this:

```
(function($) {
    $(document).ready(function() {
        // *All* project code will be written in this function
        alert("Hello jQuery!");
    });
})(jQuery);
```

10. Browse the project index page to verify jQuery is working. You should see an alert box appear displaying *Hello jQuery!*.

Add and test a click event handler which modifies its dispatching object

11. In *index.html*, locate the *button* element and notice its *id*: *showProducts*.

12. In *js/script.js*, write a *click* event handler for the *showProducts* element.

13. In the *click* event handler, open an *alert* box to test the event handler.

14. Also in the *click* event handler, use jQuery to reference *this* button which dispatched the *click* event, and set its *disabled* property to *true*.

15. Your code should look like this:

```
$(document).ready(function() {
    // *All* project code will be written in this function
    // alert("Hello jQuery!");

    $("#showProducts").click(function() {
        alert("Button clicked");
        $(this).prop("disabled", "true");
    });
});
```

16. Browse the project index page, and click the button. You should see an alert box. After closing the alert box, the button should be disabled.

17. Keep all files open.

Creating and configuring new page elements

Creating and configuring new page elements

jQuery enables creating and configuring new page elements. By convention, local variables holding jQuery objects begin with *$*.

Multiple properties can be configured by passing an inline object to the jQuery *prop()* method, with relevant attribute names and values for the element.

```
var $label = $("<p>").text("Another cat, because people look");
var $image = $("<img>").prop({
        src: "images/dieselkitty.jpg",
        width: 200});
```

Adding new elements to the page

Newly created page elements may added to the page by appending to an existing element.

Notice that tag syntax ("*<div>*") is used when creating elements, but not when selecting them.

```
// create a paragraph and image
var $label = $("<p>").text("More cats, because people look");
var $image = $("<img>").prop({
        src: "images/dieselkitty.jpg",
        width: 200});

// append these to a new div
var $item = $("<div>").append($image).append($label);

// append the created div to an existing page element named items
$("#items").append($item);
```

Assigning event handlers to newly created elements

Event handlers can be assigned to newly created elements using the *on(event, handler)* method.

```
// append these to a new div
var $item = $("<div>").append($image).append($label);
// assign an event handler to the new element
$item.on("click", function() {
        // do something
});
```

Adding and removing a CSS style

Configuring CSS styles

jQuery objects enable CSS style modification through the *css(style, value)* method, and CSS class assignment using the *addClass(classname)* method. Classes may also be alternately added and removed using the *toggleClass(classname)* method.

```
// append these to a new div
var $item = $("<div>").append($image).append($label);
// assign the CSS class named item to the new $item element
$item.addClass("item");
$item.on("click", function() {
        // toggle the CSS class named highlight when $item is clicked
        $(this).toggleClass("highlight");
});
```

Accessing and using JSON data

Understanding JSON

JSON (JavaScript Object Notation) is a data format using JavaScript object and array notation to describe data sets in external files.

```
// saved in an external file such as data/products.json
[
        {"product" : "Buttons", "price" : "2.95", "image" : "buttons.jpg"},
        {"product" : "Flowers", "price" : "4.95", "image" : "flowers.jpg"}
]
```

Loading remote data

jQuery can load and parse JSON data using its *$.getJSON(path, result handler)* function.

```
$.getJSON('data/products.json', function(data) {

});
```

Parsing and using JSON data

Returned data is parsed into JavaScript variables, of whatever structure the JSON document defines, and then passed as an argument to a result event handler.

If *data* argument is a collection (an array), it may be looped using the jQuery *each(collection, handler)* function. The each loop receives each item and its index as arguments.

```
$.getJSON('data/products.json', function(data) {
        $.each(data, function(i, item) {
                addItem(item.product, item.price, item.image);
        });
});
```

Exercise: Surveying jQuery Fundamentals - **Part 2**

In this two-part exercise you will configure a page to create and display an element for each item in an externally loaded data collection.

After completion of Part 2, you should have a basic understanding of how to:

- Use jQuery to create, configure, and add page elements

- Use jQuery to load and display external data

NOTE: This exercise quickly covers many techniques to provide an initial overview of using jQuery. All topics in this exercise are discussed in much further detail throughout the course.

Steps

Create, configure, add new page elements

1. Return to the files used in Part 1 of this exercise.

2. Below the *click* event handler, declare a *function addItem* which receives three arguments: *product*, *price*, and *image*.

3. In *addItem(product, price, image)*, use jQuery to create a *new p* element named *$label*, and assign *product* and *price* as its *text*, separated by a literal colon and dollar sign.

4. Create a new *img* element named *$image*, and assign it two properties:

   - *src: "images/" + image*

   - *width: 200*

5. Your code should look like this:

```
...
// $(this).prop("disabled", "true");
});
function addItem(product, price, image) {
    var $label = $("<p>").text(product + ": $" + price);
    var $image = $("<img>").prop({
        src: "images/" + image,
        width: 200
    });
...
```

6. In *css/style.css*, add two new CSS classes named *item* and *highlight*, configured as shown:

```
.item {
    float: left;
    padding: 10px;
}
.highlight {
    background-color: grey;
}
```

7. In *js/script.js*, create a *new div* element named *$item*, and *append* to it the *$label* and *$image* elements created above.

8. in *addItem(...)*, add the *item* class to the *$item* element.

9. Add an event handler *on $item* so *click* events will toggle the *highlight* class on *this* particular item which has been clicked.

10. Append the complete *$item* element to the *div* element with the *id items*.

11. Your complete *addItem(...)* function should look like this:

```
function addItem(product, price, image) {
    var $label = $("<p>").text(product + ": $" + price);
    var $image = $("<img>").prop({
        src: "images/" + image,
        width: 200
    });
    var $item = $("<div>").append($image).append($label);
    $item.addClass("item");
    $item.on("click", function() {
        $(this).toggleClass("highlight");
    });
    $("#items").append($item);
}
```

12. In the *showProducts click* event handler, call *addItem(...)* passing the literal strings *Buttons*, *2.95*, and *buttons.jpg* as its arguments.

```
$("#showProducts").click(function() {
    // alert("Button clicked");
    $(this).prop("disabled", "true");
    addItem("Buttons", "2.95", "buttons.jpg");
});
```

13. Browse the project index page and click the button. You should see an item appear in the display area, and the button should be disabled.

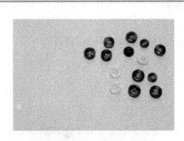

Buttons: $2.95

Load external data, and create items for each object in its collection

14. Open and review this file:

    /ftjq/2-jq-fundamentals/data/products.json

15. In *js/script.js*, below the *addItem(...)* function, declare a *function getProducts*.

16. In *getProducts()*, use the jQuery *getJSON* method to request *data/products.json*, and pass the resulting *data* to an inline event handler *function*.

17. Your code should look like this:

```
function getProducts() {
        $.getJSON('data/products.json', function(data) {

        });
}
```

18. In the *data* event handler, use jQuery to loop over *each item* in the data collection.

19. Pass the *produce*, *price*, and *image* values for each *item* to the *addItem(...)* function.

20. Your code should look like this:

```
function getProducts() {
        $.getJSON('data/products.json', function(data) {
                $.each(data, function(i, item) {
                        addItem(item.product, item.price, item.image);
                });
        });
}
```

21. In the *showProducts click* event handler, comment out the *addImage(...)* function, and replace it with a call to *getProducts()*.

```
$("#showProducts").click(function() {
        // alert("Button clicked");
        $(this).prop("disabled", "true");
        // addItem("Buttons", "2.95", "buttons.jpg");
        getProducts();
});
```

22. Browse the project index page and click the button. You should see an item displayed for each object in the *products.json* data collection.

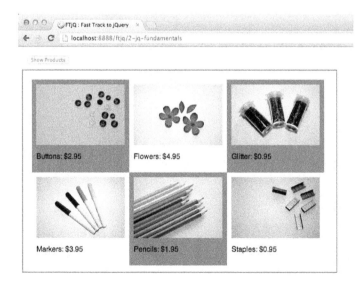

23. Close all project files.

Summary

In this unit you have learned:

- jQuery is a JavaScript library which may be deployed via CDN

- All use is controlled by the *jQuery()* function, or its shorthand symbol *$*

- A new shorthand symbol may be assigned, and scope can be controlled, by a closure

- jQuery code is normally written with a *$(document).ready* event handler

- Page elements are accessed by passing selectors to the jQuery function and using the methods of the resulting jQuery objects

- Page elements can have their *text()* and *prop()* values modified

- Page elements can have *css()* properties modified or classes assigned using *addClass()*

- Event handlers can be assigned to existing page elements through a jQuery object

- Newly created elements can have event handlers assigned using *on(event, function)*

- You can *append()* a new page element to an existing element

Review

1. Why would you wrap your jQuery code with this?

```
(function($) {

})(jQuery);
```

2. How would you assign a *click* event handler to a newly created *button*?

3. What is different between using $("*div*") and $("*<div>*")?

4. Describe how you could use jQuery to change a text font by clicking on a paragraph.

5. Imagine three uses for JSON data.

Unit 3
Traversing elements with selectors

Objectives

After completing this unit, you should understand:

- Using selectors to query the page for desired elements
- Using CSS style selectors in the jQuery function
- Selecting by HTML attributes
- Using jQuery selector extensions
- Combining selectors
- Accessing and modifying selected elements

Introducing the page query paradigm

Interacting with the page

Visualizing the document elements

HTML pages can be visualized as a tree of elements, with the HTML node as the root. It may be useful to modify all or any of these nodes in response to user or system driven events:

- display new information by adding nodes or modifying text
- guide user behavior by changing visual styles and attributes
- respond to user input and interactions

```
▼<html>
  ▼<head>
    <title>FTjQ : Fast Track to jQuery</title>
    <link rel="stylesheet" type="text/css" href="css/style.css">
  </head>
  ▼<body>
    ▼<div class="container">
      ▼<div class="controlBar">
        <button id="showProducts" disabled>Show Products</button>
      </div>
      ▼<div id="items" class="display">
        ▼<div class="item">
          <img src="images/buttons.jpg" width="200">
          <p>Buttons: $2.95</p>
        </div>
        ►<div class="item">…</div>
        ►<div class="item">…</div>
        ►<div class="item">…</div>
        ►<div class="item">…</div>
        ►<div class="item">…</div>
      </div>
      <script type="text/javascript" src="js/jquery-1.8.3.js"></script>
      <script type="text/javascript" src="js/script.js"></script>
    </div>
  </body>
</html>
```

Recalling the legacy Document Object Models

Various ways to interact with nodes as objects evolved over the history of web browsing. The World Wide Web Consortium (W3C) has developed and promoted ECMAScript (standardized JavaScript, 1997) and three DOM standards, to date.

- *"DOM Level 0"*: 1996 (pre-W3C), arbitrary browser capabilities
- *DOM Level 1*: 1998 (W3C), complete model for HTML documents
- *DOM Level 2*: 2000 (W3C), event model and *getElementById()* function
- *DOM Level 3*: 2004 (W3C), XPath queries and keyboard events
- *DOM Level 4*: not yet final

http://www.w3.org/DOM/

http://xml.coverpages.org/dom.html

Legacy element access

```
// get reference to a named button
var mybutton = document.getElementById("mybutton");

// get reference to first paragraph in third div in the document
var para1 = document.getElementByTagName("div")[2].getElementByTagName("p")[0];
```

Minimizing traversal code using page queries

Introducing query based selection

CSS selectors (class, id, tag) are a widely understood way to reference page elements. This approach is now being implemented in JavaScript to select object references.

The emerging query-selector approach is supported by most newer browsers:

```
var myButton = document.querySelector("#mybutton");

var myHighlights = document.querySelectorAll(".highlight");

var myHighlightedImages = document.querySelectorAll("img.highlight");
```

These methods are becoming widely supported, but are not universal. The CanIUse.com site is useful in understanding and accomodating browser compatibility issues.

http://caniuse.com/queryselector

Understanding the value of jQuery

jQuery is an evolving, actively maintained framework supporting query-selector based page element selection, traversal, and modification.

But, as a framework built <u>on</u> JavaScript, it:

- abstracts away cross-browser incompatibilities

- adds functionality not yet standardized, much less implemented in all browsers

Like the evolving *querySelector(selector)* and *querySelectorAll(selector)* methods, jQuery supports querying for elements based on CSS selectors, but with compact syntax and added capabilities.

Selecting page elements

Introducing element selection

Understanding jQuery selector syntax

By default, the jQuery function searches the full document tree for matching elements

```
// select all divs in the page and assign the resulting jQuery object
var allDivs = $("div");
```

By default, the jQuery function searches the full document tree for matching elements

```
// when user mouses over the div assigned the id 'mainStory', search its child
// elements (only) for paragraphs of class 'important', and italicize them

$("div#mainStory").mouseover(function() {
        var $importantParas = $("p.important", this);
        $importantParas.css("font-style", "italic");
});
```

jQuery statements are commonly chained

```
$("p.important", this).css("font-style", "italic");
```

Using CSS selectors

Using class, id, and tag selectors

Class

```
// change the color of all elements assigned the highlight class
$(".highlight").css("background-color", "red");
```

ID

```
// disable the submit button
$("#mySubmit").prop("disabled", "true");
```

Tag

```
// hide all paragraphs on the page
$("p").hide();
```

Using span and div to mark content for manipulation

Clearly identified elements are easy to select. In addition to assigning *id* and *class* values to specific elements, *div* and *span* elements can be used to mark page content for manipulation.

A *div* is a block element, which takes page space. A *span* is an inline element which enables content tagging, but has no visual effect of its own.

```
<div class="item office sale">
  <img src="images/pencils.jpg" width="200" />
  <p><span id="itemName">Pencils</span>:<span id="itemPrice">$1.95</span></p>
</div>
```

Understanding id vs. class selectors

Assigning an *id* implies its element is unique within a page or variable scope.

Assigning a *class* implies its element belongs to a category - a "class" - of related objects within a page or variable scope.

While the same results can sometimes be achieved in both CSS and JavaScript / JQuery by re-using an *id* rather than a *class*, it is a bad practice, and may lead to problems in jQuery and other frameworks, which assume *id* values are used correctly.

```
<div id="displayContainer"></div>
<div id="displayContainer"></div>

<div id="container1" class="display"></div>
<div id="container2" class="display"></div>
```

Using tag, id, and class selectors in combination

Tags of a specified class

```
$("div.left_col").css("font-weight", "bold");
```

Elements with two specified classes

```
$(".menuItem.vegetarian").show();
```

Specified ID if a particular class has been assigned

```
$("#myButton.formValid").prop("disabled", "false");
```

Exercise: Playing with jQuery CSS selection

In this exercise you will use tag, id, and class selectors individually and in combination to select and modify page elements.

After completion, you should be able to:

- Select page elements using tag, class, and id selectors with the jQuery function

- Begin to use CSS class attributes to categorize page information

Steps

Review project files

1. Open the following project and review its starting HTML and CSS files:

    `/ftjq/3-selector-play`

2. Specifically notice the *id* and *class* values associated with its various *div* elements.

    - *ids:* container1, container2

    - *classes:* item, office, home, sale

3. Browse the *index.html* page to see its default visual state, with *item* elements that have the *office, home,* and/or *sale* classes assigned to them.

Use id selector to create click event handler

4. Open the *js/script.js* file.

5. In the correct area of the script, use an *id* selector for the *selectElements* button to create a *click* event handler.

6. In the *click* event handler, open an *alert* box to indicate the *button* was clicked.

7. Your code should look like this:

```
$(document).ready(function () {

        $("#selectElements").click(function() {
               alert("Click!");
        })

});
```

8. Refresh the page, click the button, and verify its event handler is working.

Use tag selector to move all images

9. In *js/script.js*, comment out the *alert* function.

10. Use the jQuery function to select all *img* tags, and assign the resulting jQuery object to a local *var* named *$images*.

11. Call the *appendTo(selector)* method on the *$images* jQuery object, and target the *div* with the *id container2*.

12. Your code should look like this:

```
$("#selectElements").click(function() {
        // alert("Click!");

        var $images = $("img");
        $images.appendTo("#container2");

});
```

13. Refresh the page, click the button, and you should see the images removed from the *item div* elements, and appended to the *container2 div*.

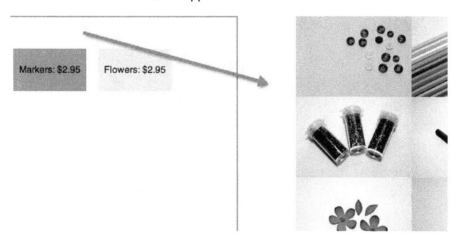

14. In *js/script.js*, modify your code to *clone()* the *$images* prior to appending them.

```
$("#selectElements").click(function() {
        // alert("Click!");

        var $images = $("img");
        $images.clone().appendTo("#container2");

});
```

15. Refresh the page, click the button, and you should see the images appended to *container2* with the original *item* images left intact.

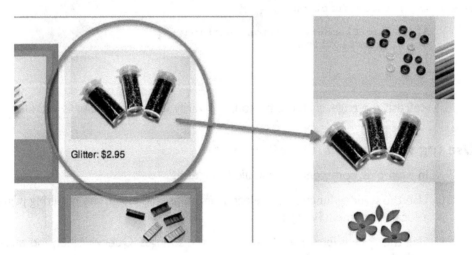

User class selector to move all items

16. In *js/script.js*, comment out the previous select and append statements.

17. Using one statement, select all elements of class *item*, and append them to *container2*.

18. Your code should look like this:

```
$("#selectElements").click(function() {
    ...
    $(".item").appendTo("#container2");
});
```

19. Refresh the page, click, and you should see all *item* divs move to the *container2 div*.

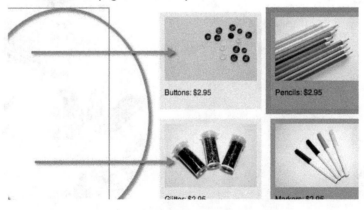

Use selectors to move specific items

20. In *js/script.js*, comment out the previous jQuery statement.

21. Modify your code to select only *office* class *div* elements and move them to *container2*.

```
$("#selectElements").click(function() {
    ...
    // $(".item").appendTo("#container2");
    $("div.office").appendTo("#container2");
});
```

22. Refresh the page, click, and you should see only *office* divs move to *container2*.

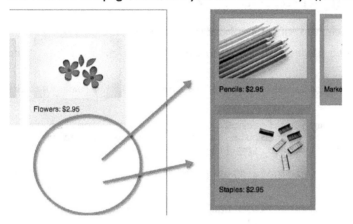

23. In *js/script.js*, comment out the previous jQuery statement.

24. Modify your code to change the background color of *sale* items to *#cf4d47*.

```
$("#selectElements").click(function() {
    ...
    // $("div.office").appendTo("#container2");
    $(".item.sale").css("background-color", "#cf4d47")
});
```

25. Refresh the page, click, and *sale* items only should turn completely red.

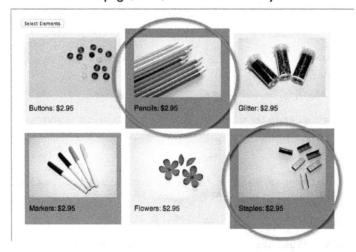

26. Close all project files.

Adding precision to page queries

Using HTML attribute selectors

Selecting by an element's attribute or its value

Attribute selectors follow this general syntax. The preceding element reference, and the comparison to a specified value, are both optional.

```
$("element-name[attribute-name='value']");
```

Elements may be selected for an attribute or attribute value

```
// use no element reference, so select all elements with a 'src' attribute
$("[src]");

// use an element reference, so select only 'div' elements having a 'width'
$("div[width]");

// use both an element reference and compare to value, so select only 'img'
// elements with a 'src' attribute assigned a specified value
$("img[src='images/buttons.jpg']");

// select all 'div' elements with a 'width' attribute of 200
$("div[width='200']");

// select the form input field named "firstName"
$("input[name='fieldName']");
```

Qualifying HTML attribute values

Using attribute qualifiers in selectors

Selected attribute values may be qualified with these operators:

- not   !=

```
// select 'img' elements which do not have a 'width' attribute of 200
$("img[width!='200']");
```

- begins   ^=

```
// select all elements with a 'src' beginning with 'images'
$("[src^='images']");
```

- ends $=

```
// select all 'img' elements with a 'src' ending with 'jpg'
$("img[src$='jpg']");
```

- contains   *=

```
// select all 'a' elements with a 'href' containing 'figleaf.com'
$("a[href*='figleaf.com']");
```

- contains word   ~=

```
// select all 'div' elements assigned the 'home' class
$("div[class~='home']");
// note, same selection could be made as $("div.home");
```

Dynamically building a selector

Building a selector as a string

Attribute selectors may be built as a string, then assigned

```
var path = "images/buttons.jpg";
var selector = "[src='" + path + "']";

var $selections = $(selector);
```

Building a selector from user-chosen values

Commonly, HTML select elements may be used in creating a dynamic jQuery selector. The value of an element may be accessed using a jQuery object's *val()* method. In an event handler, the *this* keyword refers to the object dispatching the event.

```
...
<select id="selectCategory">
      <option value="office">Office</option>
      <option value="home">Home</option>
      <option value="sale">Sale</option>
</select>
...
$("#selectCategory").change(function() {
      var chosenCategory = $(this).val();
      // select elements with both 'item' class and the selected class
      var selector = ".item." + chosenCategory + ")";
      $(selector).show();
});
```

Using jQuery selector extensions

Introducing jQuery selector extensions

jQuery enables a large set of specialized selector extensions, which follow this general syntax. The element name is optional. Only some of the jQuery extensions accept arguments.

$("***element-name*:extension(*argument*)**");

:animated	:button	:checkbox	:checked	:contains(text)
:disabled	:empty	:enabled	:eq(index)	:even
:file	:first	:first-child	:gt(index)	:has(selector)
:header	:hidden	:image	:input	:last
:last-child	:lt(index)	:not(selector)	:nth(index)	:nth-child(index)
:odd	:only-child	:parent	:password	:radio
:reset	:selected	:submit	:text	:visible

Exploring jQuery selector extensions

Some examples using jQuery selector extensions are given below, and used in context throughout the course.

```
// select all 'input' elements which are buttons
$("input:button");
// note, $(":button") is also valid, but slower because less specific

// change background color of even-numbered table rows green
$("tr:even").css("background-color", "#00FF00");

// strike through the text of of the 6th and higher table rows
// note, index value is zero-based
$("tr:gt(4)").css("text-decoration", "line-through");

// turn table rows grey unless assigned the 'total' class
$("tr:not('.total')").css("background-color, "grey");

// select the table cell (td) containing the word "Buttons"
$("td:contains('Buttons')");
```

Detailed descriptions of each jQuery selector extension may be found here:

http://api.jquery.com/category/selectors/jquery-selector-extensions/

Combining and grouping selectors

Using jQuery selectors in combination

Any number of jQuery selectors may be used in combination to provide more specificity. More specific selectors generally result in faster selection on the page. Combined selectors are processed from left to right.

- any descendant element   *A   B*

```
// all odd table rows in the table with id 'tickets'
$("#tickets tr:odd");
```

- direct child element   *A > B*

```
// direct children of any class 'item' element that are a div with id 'price'
$(".item > div#price");
```

- immediately following sibling   *A + B*

```
// sibling div immediately following the div with id 'price'
$("div#price + *");
```

- any following sibling   *A ~ B*

```
// any sibling div after a div with id 'price' that has the class 'description'
$("div#price ~ div.description");
```

Exploring combined jQuery selectors

Combined jQuery selectors are used in context throughout the course. An example might be:

```
// log user's selected options from the select control with id 'category'
...
<select id="category" multiple="multiple">
      <option value="office">Office</option>
      <option value="home">Home</option>
      <option value="sale">Sale</option>
</select>
...
$("#category option:selected").each(function() {
      console.log($(this).val());
})
```

```
// select all immediate child p elements of div elements with class 'price'
$("div.price > p");
```

Selecting groups of elements

A comma-separated list of selectors can be specified. All matching elements are returned in the resulting collection of jQuery objects.

```
// select all h1, h2, and h3 elements
$("h1, h2, h3");
```

```
// select all divs with either the 'price' or 'description' class
$("div.price, div.description");
```

```
// select the header and footer elements
$("header, footer");
```

Accessing selected elements

Treating the query results like an array

As discussed, passing a selector to the jQuery function returns a collection of zero or more jQuery objects. Methods are available to access objects in this collection.

- $(selector).*length*

- $(selector).*first()*

- $(selector).*last()*

```
// log the first, last, and total number of p elements in div#article
var $paragraphs = $("div#article > p");
console.log($paragraphs.first());
console.log($paragraphs.last());
console.log("Total paragraph count: " + $paragraphs.length);
```

- $(selector).*eq(index)*

- $(selector)*[index]*

```
// log the same third paragraph, two different ways, assuming all p elements
// are immediate children of div#article
console.log($("div#article p").eq(2));
console.log($("div#article > p")[2]);
```

- $(selector).*slice(inclusive start index, non-inclusive end index)*

```
// log the third, fourth, and fifth paragraphs
console.log($("div#article p").slice(2,5));
```

Excluding specified elements from the results

The jQuery function supports a *.not(selector)* method to exclude elements from the results returned by the main selector.

```
// return all div element except those with id 'header' or 'footer'
$("div").not("#header, #footer");
```

Looping over each selected element

jQuery objects support an *each(function)* method which passes each object in the selected collection to a function, along with its index position.

```
// return the category options the user did not select, then loop over each
// returned object and display its value using the 'this' keyword
...
<select id="category" multiple="multiple">
     <option value="office">Office</option>
     <option value="home">Home</option>
     <option value="sale">Sale</option>
</select>
...
$("select#category option").not(":selected").each(function() {
     // do something to each object
});
```

Inside the *.each()* function, elements can be accessed by selecting this with the *this* keyword.

```
// return the category options the user did not select, then loop over each
// returned object and display its value using the 'this' keyword
...
<select id="category" multiple="multiple">
     <option value="office">Office</option>
     <option value="home">Home</option>
     <option value="sale">Sale</option>
</select>
...
$("select#category option").not(":selected").each(function() {
     console.log($(this).val());
});
```

Alternately, arguments are passed to the *.each()* function, exposing each elements and its index.

```
// return the category options the user did not select, then loop over each
// returned object and display both its index and value using the arguments
...
<select id="category" multiple="multiple">
     <option value="office">Office</option>
     <option value="home">Home</option>
     <option value="sale">Sale</option>
</select>
...
$("select#category option").not(":selected").each(function(index, element) {
     console.log("Element #: " + index);
     console.log($(element).val();)
});
```

Examining and manipulating jQuery objects

jQuery objects support an API for examining and modifying their values, and referencing their related elements.

The .hasClass(class) method returns *true* if the element represented by a jQuery object has the specified class.

```
$("div.item").each(function(index, element) {
        if($(element).hasClass("office")) {
                console.log(index + " is an office item.");
        }
});
```

The .parent() method references the immediate parent of the element represented by the jQuery object.

```
// turn the row containing the 'total' cell red
$("#cart td.total").parent().css("background-color", "#ff0000");
```

jQuery methods are discussed in more detail further in the course.

Exercise: Using complex selectors and accessing their results

In this exercise you will use complex selectors to manipulate elements in response to events

After completion, you should be able to:

- Select for odd numbered elements, and items excluding a specified class

- Iterate over each element in a collection of jQuery objects

- Use the *.hasClass(class)*, *.not(class)*, and *.filter(selector)* methods on jQuery objects

Steps

Review project files

1. Open the following project and review its starting HTML and CSS files:

   `/ftjq/3-complex-selectors`

2. In *index.html*, pecifically notice the *id* and *class* values associated with its various *div, table,* and *tr* elements.

   - *ids:* container, controlBar, categories, items, cart

   - *classes:* item home office sale total

3. Browse the *index.html* page, to view the initial state of the page.

4. In *js/script.js*, review the pre-built *.ready()* and *.change()* event handlers.

Modify table row CSS at startup

5. In *js/script.js*, select the *:odd* table rows in the *#cart* table, and set their background color to *#c0f0b1* at application startup.

```
jQuery(document).ready(function () {
      $("#cart tr:odd").css("background-color", "#c9f0b1");
      ...
```

6. Browse the *index.html* page, and you should see alternating row colors.

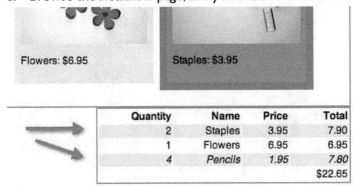

Note: This is an anti-pattern. The same effect could be created using CSS. Whenever possible, use CSS, as it renders more quickly. See commented code in css/style.css to achieve this effect without JavaScript.

Toggle CSS on table row events specified by jQuery selector extension

7. Add a *.click()* event handler for table row (*tr*) tags in the *#cart table*.

8. Add a jQuery selector extension so *tr* tags with the *.total* class are *:not* selected when adding the event handlers.

9. In *css/style.css*, review the *.highlight* rule.

10. When a *click* event is dispatched on any selected *tr*, toggle the *highlight* class on the *tr* dispatching the event.

11. Your code should look like this:

```
$("#cart tr:not('.total')").click(function() {
      $(this).toggleClass("highlight");
});
```

Note: CSS class names must include "." and id names must include "#" when used in selectors (even if they must be concatenated), but not when passed to jQuery methods.

12. Browse *index.html*, and click on *#cart* table rows. Clicking should toggle the rows between normal and italic text. The effect should <u>not</u> work on the header row, or the last row with the *.total* class.

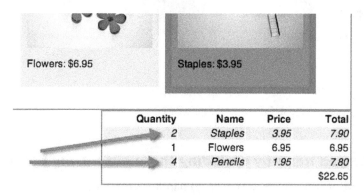

Update items using .each() and .hasClass()

13. In *js/script.js*, in the *.change()* handler for the *#categories* select control, select all *.item div* elements, and pass *.each()* to a function which receives the *index* and *element* as arguments.

14. Assign the *.val()* of the *#categories* select control to a local *var* named *category*.

15. If the category value is "*all*", or if the current element has the selected category as one of its classes, then *.show()* the current element, otherwise *.hide()* the current element.

16. Your code should look like this:

```
$("#categories").change(function() {
...
    $(".item").each(function(index, element){
        var category = $("#categories").val();
        if (category === "all" || $(element).hasClass(category)) {
            $(element).show();
        } else {
            $(element).hide();
        }
    });
...
```

17. Browse *index.html*. Selecting *All*, *Office*, *Home*, or *Sale* should update the display.

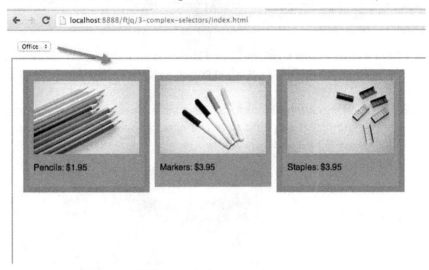

Update displayed items by excluding those not having the selected class

18. Comment out the *$(".item").each(...)* handler written the prior section.

19. In the *.change()* handler for the *#categories* select control, show all *div* elements of the *.item* class.

20. Assign the *.val()* of *this* select control, which is having its *change* event handled, to a local *var* named *category*.

21. *If* the category is not *"all"*, then select all *div* elements of the *.item* class, excluding those which are *.not()* of the current *category*, and *.hide()* them.

22. Your code should look like this:

```
$("#categories").change(function() {
...
    $("div.item").show();
    var category = $(this).val();
    if (category !== "all") {
        $("div.item").not("." + category).hide();
    }
...
```

Note: when referencing a CSS class as a selector, it must include a "." prefix.

23. Browse *index.html*. Selecting *All*, *Office*, *Home*, or *Sale* should update the display.

(Optional) Update displayed items assigning a filter for those having the selected class

24. Common out the code written in the prior section.

25. Select and assign all *div* elements of the *.item* class to a local *var $items*.

26. Call the *.hide()* method on *$items*.

27. Assign the *.val()* of *this* select control to a local *var* named *category*.

28. Using a ternary operator on a self-executing boolean expression, if *category* is *not* "*all*" then *.filter()* the *$items* for the *category* and *.show()* the result, else *.show()* all *$items*.

29. Your code should look like this:

```
var $items = $("div.item");
$items.hide();
var category = $(this).val();
(category !== "all") ? $items.filter("." + category).show() : $items.show();
```

30. Browse *index.html*. Selecting *All*, *Office*, *Home*, or *Sale* should update the display.

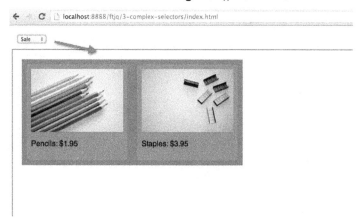

31. Close all files for this project.

Summary

In this unit you have learned:

- Modern JavaScript modifies pages by selecting for desired elements

- CSS tag, id, and class selectors may be used individually or in combination to select elements using the jQuery function

- HTML attributes and their values, such as $("img[width != '200']"), may be used as part of selecting elements

- jQuery provides selector extensions, such as :odd, :button, and :not(selector), to select elements with desired states or values

- The jQuery function exposes methods, such as .not() and .filter(), to modify selected element collections

- Elements matching the selection criteria are returned as a collection of jQuery objects, which may be manipulated and iterated similar to an array, with methods such as .first() and .each().

Review

1. Describe ways you could select for *img* elements loaded from a folder of *JPG* files named "*photos*", which have each been assigned a *.vacation* class, and displayed with a *width* of 200?

2. Describe ways you could select for all password controls in a page.

3. How could you disable a button which has the id #submit?

4. Describe ways to select all table rows except those assigned the *.subtotal* class.

5. If both approaches are possible, should you modify the page appearance using jQuery or directly with CSS? Why?

Unit 4
Modifying selected properties and styles

Objectives

After completing this unit, you should understand:

- Getting and setting element properties

- Setting and accessing custom element data

- Modifying display by assigning new text or HTML content

Introducing property modification

Reviewing DOM node structure

An HTML document is a tree of nodes. The DOM recognizes several node types, including:

- *Document*: root node, one per page

- *Element*: each individual HTML element ("tag")

- *Text*: text nested within an element

- *Attribute*: name/value pairs assigned to an element (e.g., *href, src, width*, etc.)

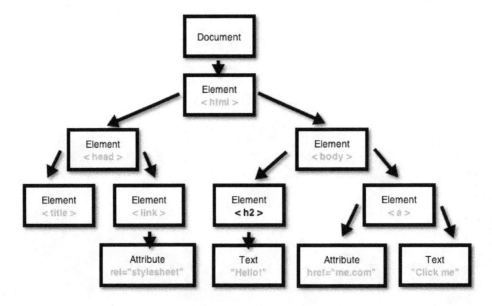

Introducing five main ways to change an element

There are five main ways to modify a selected element:

1. change its HTML attributes
2. change its child text node
3. change its child or parent HTML node(s)
4. change its CSS styles
5. change its geometry, either size or position

jQuery objects expose methods for modifying any of these values. The HTML, text, and CSS ways are discussed in this unit. The rest are discussed later in this course.

Understanding "property" vs. "attribute"

The DOM can be ambiguous. Sometimes the value of an attribute is significant, and sometimes the mere existence of an attribute is significant.

```
<!-- browsers render these the same way -->
<input id="mycheckbox" type="checkbox" checked />
<input id="mycheckbox" type="checkbox" checked="checked" />
```

For simplicity, jQuery 1.6+ terminology focuses on getting and setting the "properties" of a jQuery object, in favor of accessing its "attributes". As a result, two very commonly used methods function identically in nearly all situations.

```
// Older jQuery Code
$("#mycheckbox").attr("checked", "true");        // set attribute
var checked = $("#mycheckbox").attr("checked");  // get attribute

// New jQuery Code (1.6+)
$("#mycheckbox").prop("checked", "true");        // set property
var checked = $("#mycheckbox").prop("checked");  // get property
```

In line with jQuery's evolution, this course focuses on using the *.prop()* method over *.attr()*, but in virtually all situations their use is interchangeable.

Modifying jQuery object properties

Understanding jQuery get/set methods

Getting and setting element properties

jQuery uses the *.prop(name [, value])* method to both get and set values.

```
// get and assign current property value to checked as a string
var checked = $("#mycheckbox").prop("checked");

// set a new property value
$("#mycheckbox").prop("checked", "true");
```

Getting and setting properties on jQuery object collections

If a selector returns multiple objects, you:

- get the value of the <u>first</u> matching element

```
<img src="buttons.jpg" />
<img src="pencils.jpg" />
...
// get path of first image, of all img elements on the page
var path = $("img").prop("src");
console.log(path); // logs buttons.jpg
```

- set the value of <u>all</u> matching elements

```
// set path of the all img elements on the page
$("img").prop("src", "buttons.jpg"); // all images update to buttons.jpg
```

Assigning multiple or calculated properties

Setting multiple properties using an object

Multiple element properties may be set simultaneously by passing an object to the *.prop()* method. The object may be written inline as an object literal, or constructed separately.

```
// assign multiple img properties inline
$("#saleitem").prop({    src:"staples.jpg",
                         alt:"Staple on sale!",
                         width:"200", height:"150" });

// assign multiple img properties by object
var saleimage = {   src:"staples.jpg",
                    alt:"Staple on sale!",
                    width:"200", height:"150" };

$("#saleitem").prop(saleimage);
```

Calculating properties by function

Because JavaScript functions are objects, they may be passed to the *.prop(name, value)* method to calculate the value of an assigned property.

```
<a href="http://www.figleaf.com">Figleaf</a>
<a href="index.html">Home</a>
...
// load all onsite links in same window, offsite links in new window
$("a").prop("target", function() {
        if(this.host === location.host) {
                return "_self";
        } else {
                return "_blank";
        }
});
```

Interacting with element content

Manipulating text content

Manipulating and using element text

Elements supporting text content - such as *h1*, *div*, *a*, *p*, and so on - can be read or modified using the *.text([string])* method.

```
// get text from #banner1
var banner1text = $("#banner1").text();

// assign text to #banner2
$("#banner2").text(banner1text);
```

Combining text manipulation with selectors and events enables dynamic page updates.

```
<h2 id="messageBar">Welcome to the store!</h2>
...
<div class="sale">
    <img src="pencils.jpg" width="200" />
    <span id="name">Pencils</span>: <span id="price">$1.95</span>
</div>
<div class="sale">
    <img src="buttons.jpg" width="200" />
    <span id="name">Buttons</span>: <span id="price">$2.95</span>
</div>
...
// when mousing over .sale items, display message with item name in #messageBar
$(".sale").mouseover(function() {
    // use this keyword to provide correct context for selecting #name
    var name = $("#name", this).text();
    // set dynamic text string in #messageBar
    $("#messageBar").text("Sale on " + name + "!");
});
```

Note, without adding the this keyword to the $("#name", this) selector, you would read the .text() of the first page element with that selected id, instead of the particular one dispatching the mouseover event.

Manipulating HTML content

Understanding adding text vs. HTML content

Assigning text to an element adds to it a single child *Text* node. Adding HTML to an element, though, potentially adds an entire new tree of *HTML* and *Text* nodes. So, HTML is added using a different method than text.

```
$("#messageBar").text("Sale on now!");
```

```
$("#messageBar").html("<p>Sale on now!</p>");
```

Configuring elements with HTML content

Elements supporting HTML content can be read or modified using the *.html([string])* method.

```
// get HTML from #banner1
var banner1HTML = $("#banner1").html();

// assign HTML to #banner2
$("#banner2").html("<h2>New items in stock!</h2>");
```

Manipulating element data

Assigning data properties to elements

Arbitrary data properties may be assigned to almost any element, using the *.data(name, value)* method.

```
// assign an inventory count for a displayed item
$("#buttons").data("inventory", "83");

// retrieve and display an available inventory count
var inventory = $("#buttons").data("inventory");
$("#available").text(available); // displays 83
```

Due to cross-browser issues, data cannot be assigned to XML documents using this method (XML is parsed and manipulated using XML specific methods).

Assigning objects as element data

Each property of an object passed to the *.data(object)* method will be created as its own name/value pair of that element's data.

```
// assign multiple element data items using an object
var itemData = {inventory: "83", discount:"75"};
$("#buttons").data(itemData);

// access and assign data to local variable
var inventory = $("#buttons").data("inventory");
$("#available").text(inventory); // displays 83

// directly access assigned data
$("#available").text( $("#buttons").data().inventory ); // displays 83
```

Recall that constructor functions may be used to create objects.

```
function Item(inventory, discount) {
      this.inventory = inventory;
      this.discount = discount;
}

// assign element data using a constructor function
$("#buttons").data(new Item("83", ".75"));

// access assigned data
$("#available").text( $("#buttons").data().inventory ); // displays 83
```

Functions, arrays, and other JavaScript object types may be serialized and stored as data.

Understanding how jQuery tracks custom data

jQuery stores element data in its *jQuery.cache* property, keyed to a unique ID which adds to any element to which data has been assigned.

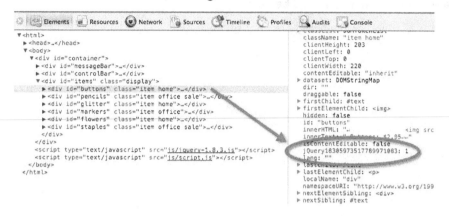

Exercise: Modifying and using element text, data, and HTML

In this exercise you will get and set element properties and data to customize the display in response to the user's interaction with visual items.

After completion, you should be able to:

- Get and set selected element properties

- Assign custom data to an element using a constructed object

- Access and use custom data to update the display

- Modify element display by assigning new text or HTML content

Steps

Review project files

1. Open the following project and review its starting HTML and CSS files:

   `/ftjq/4-modify-properties`

2. Specifically notice the new *id* values associated with its various *div* and *span* elements.

   - *div ids:* messageBar, image, message, buttons, pencils, glitter, markers, flowers, staples

   - *span ids:* name, price

3. Browse *index.html*, and notice the newly added *#messageBar* area.

Display selected image in new area

4. In *js/script.js .ready()* handler, declare a *mouseover* event handler for *.item* elements.

5. In the event handler, assign the *src* of *this img* being moused over to a local *var path*.

6. Select the *#image* element, and set its *src* property to the *path* value.

7. Your code should look like this:

```
$(".item").mouseover(function() {
    var path = $("img", this).prop("src");
    $("#image").prop("src", path);
});
```

8. Save your changes, and browse *index.html*. Roll over *.item* elements, and the image should be copied into the *#messageBar*.

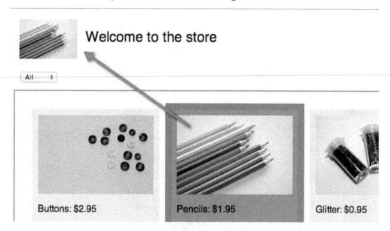

Assigning element data using an object constructor

9. Declare an *Item* constructor *function* which receives *inventory*, *price*, and *discount* arguments, and assigns them to like-named properties of *this* object of the function.

10. Select the *#buttons* elements, and assign a *new Item* object to it using its *.data()* method, with *"23"*, *"2.95"*, and *".15"* as arguments to the *Item* constructor.

11. Your code should look like this:

```
$("#buttons").data(new Item("23", "2.95", ".15"));
...
function Item(inventory, price, discount) {
    this.inventory = inventory;
    this.price = price;
    this.discount = discount;
}
```

12. Uncomment the remaining five *.data()* assignment statements.

13. Save your changes and browse the *index.html* page. Using your browser developer tools, examine the detailed properties of the *#buttons* div element. You should see a unique jQuery ID has been added to the node, enabling jQuery to track its assigned data.

Using stored element data to modify displayed text and html

14. Declare five local variables *name*, *price*, *discount*, *discountPrice*, and *priceDisplay*.

15. Select all *.item* elements, and assign them *mouseover* event handlers.

16. In the event handler, assign the value displayed within the *#name* span within *this* particular *.item* dispatching the event, and assign it to the *name* variable.

17. Your code should look like this:

```
...
var name, price, discount, discountPrice, priceDisplay;
$(".item").mouseover(function() {
      name = $("#name", this).text();

});
```

18. Below the assignment of *text* to *name*, get the value of the *price* data associated with *this* element, and assign it to the *price* variable.

19. Assign *priceDisplay* a literal dollar sign concatenated to the value of *price*.

20. Select the *#message* element, and assign the *name* and *priceDisplay* values as *text* describing the item's cost.

21. Your code should look like this:

```
...
var name, price, discount, discountPrice, priceDisplay;
$(".item").mouseover(function() {
      name = $("#name", this).text();
      price = $(this).data("price");
      priceDisplay = "$" + price;

      $("#message").text(name + " are only " + priceDisplay);

});
```

22. Save your changes, and browse *index.html*. Rolling over items should cause their name and price appear in *#messageBar*, along with their image.

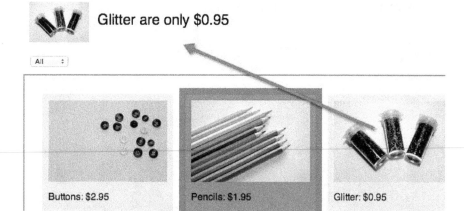

23. In the event handler, directly above the assignment of *text* to *#message*, test *if this .item* has been assigned the *sale* class.

```
...
priceDisplay = "$" + price;
if ($(this).hasClass("sale")) {

}
$("#message").text(name + " are only " + priceDisplay);
...
```

24. In the condition, access the *.data()* of this particular object and assign the value of its *discount* property to the local *discount* variable.

25. Using *price* and *discount*, calculate the discounted price to two decimals places, and assign the result to *discountPrice*.

26. Modify the *priceDisplay* variable by using concatenation to wrap its current value in a *<strike>* tag, and follow that with a literal dollar sign followed by *discountPrice*.

27. Your complete event handler should look like this:

```
var name, price, discount, discountPrice, priceDisplay;
$(".item").mouseover(function() {
  name = $("#name", this).text();
  price = $(this).data("price");
  priceDisplay = "$" + price;
  if ($(this).hasClass("sale")) {
    discount = $(this).data().discount;
    discountPrice = (price - (price * discount)).toFixed(2);
    priceDisplay = "<strike>" + priceDisplay + "</strike> $" + discountPrice;
  }
  $("#message").text(name + " are only " + priceDisplay);
});
```

28. Save your changes and browse *index.html*. Rolling over sale items should display both *price* and *discountPrice*, but the *<strike>* tag does not render properly.

 Pencils are only <strike>$1.95</strike> $1.56

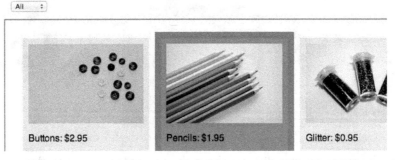

29. In the event handler, on the *#message* selector, modify your code to assign the display string to the *.html()* method rather than the *.text()* method.

```
...
  priceDisplay = "<strike>" + priceDisplay + "</strike> $" + discountPrice;
}
$("#message").html(name + " are only " + priceDisplay);
});
```

30. Save your changes and browse *index.html*. Regular prices on sale items should have a strike through.

 Pencils are only ~~$1.95~~ $1.56

31. Close all project files.

Modifying CSS styles

Understanding the need

Simplifying cross-browser distinctions

Despite years of standardization effort, browsers still implement CSS differently. For example:

	Standards Based Browsers	Microsoft Internet Explorer
Access style values	`.getComputedStyle()`	`.currentStyle` `.runtimeStyle`
Float property	`"cssFloat"`	`"styleFloat"`

jQuery exposes styles using a single term, and manages cross-browser distinctions internally. For example, jQuery accesses CSS styles using the succinct *.css()* method, and *float* values using the "*float*" property.

Describing category and identity

Interacting with CSS becomes important for behaviors beyond simple rollover effects. Also, CSS syntax plays an additional role in jQuery, because ID and Class values express individual identity and group category, as well as serving as hooks for CSS-provided visual effects.

As seen, the fact that a Product object belongs to the sale class is significant not just for setting a background color, but for determining how to calculate a displayed price.

Setting styles on selected elements

Getting and setting individual styles

Much like the *.prop(name [, value])* method, the *.css(name [, value])* method is used to both get and set the styles of a selected object.

```
// get textAlign value of first td element
textAlign = $("td").css("text-align");

// get all td elements, set textAlign right if numeric
$("td").each(function(index, item) {
        text = $(item).text();
        if ($.isNumeric(text)) {
                $(item).css("text-align", "right");
        }
});
```

When using *.css()*, individual styles may be accessed using either CSS or JavaScript naming. For example, text alignment may be accessed as either "*text-align*" or "*textAlign*".

Setting multiple styles

Styles may also be set using an object defining multiple individual styles. However, because JavaScript does not permit hyphens in names, JavaScript style naming must be used.

```
// sets multiple table styles
$("#teamTable").css({
                fontWeight: "bold",
                backgroundColor: "red"
                });
// SYNTAX ERROR: unexpected token "-"
$("#teamTable").css({
                font-weight: "bold",
                background-color: "red"
                });
```

Choosing how to set styles

Browsers apply CSS styles faster than they execute JavaScript so, where possible, styles should be assigned using standard CSS, not JavaScript or jQuery.

CSS does supports some basic interactions natively, such as *:hover* ("rollover") effects.

```
/* turn table rows yellow on rollover */
tr:hover {
        background-color: yellow;
}
```

Other interactions, such as toggling behaviors or postion-based animation, must be built with code. jQuery provides support for such behaviors.

Adding and removing classes from selected elements

Adding classes

Class are added at runtime using the *.addClass(name[name name])* method. A literal class name, list of class names (no commas), or a function which returns a name or list of names may be passed to this method as its argument.

Classes may be assigned to elements <u>whether or not</u> they are defined in a related CSS file.

```
.highlight { font-style: bold; background-color: yellow }
/* note: no bonus class defined in CSS */
...
<button id="showBonus">Show Bonus</button>
<input type="text" name="bonusName" />
<table id="teamTable">
  <tr><td>Vern Violet</td><td>23</td></tr>
  <tr><td>Krishna Kohl</td><td>42</td></tr>
</table>
...
// assign bonus to any field containing the provided name, and add highlight
$("#showBonus").click(function() {
        bonusName = $("input[name='bonusName']").val();
        $("tr:contains('" + bonusName + "')").addClass("bonus");
        $("tr.bonus").addClass("highlight");

        // alternate approach to same effect
        // $("tr:contains('" + bonusName + "')").addClass("bonus highlight");
});
```

Note, classes are useful to categorize elements for informational reasons, not simply to assign visual styles. Having distinct informational and visual classes such as .bonus and .highlight may be helpful.

Removing classes

Class are removed at runtime using the *.removeClass(name[name name])* method. A literal class name, list of class names (no commas), or a function which returns a name or list of names may be passed to this method as its argument.

```
// clear the bonuses from the displayed rows and remove the highlight
$("#clearTable").click(function() {
        $("tr").removeClass("bonus highlight");
});
```

Toggling classes

Classes may be toggled - added if missing, removed if there - using *.toggleClass(name [name, name])*. A literal class name, list of class names (no commas), or a function which returns a name or list of names may be passed to this method as its argument.

```
$("#toggleBonus").on("click", function() {
        $("tr.bonus").toggleClass("highlight");
});
```

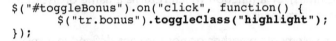

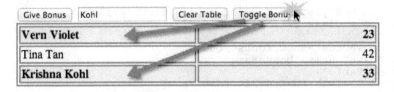

Note, .on("click", function() {...}) is the method which the shorthand version .click(function() {...}) relies on internally. Event handlers are discussed in more detail later in the course.

Testing elements for classes

Checking whether an element has been assigned a class

The *.hasClass(name)* method returns true if its target has been assigned the specified class.

```
...
<tr class="manager"><td>Tina Tan</td><td>42</td></tr>
...
$("tr").each(function(index, item) {
        if($(item).hasClass("manager")) {
                $(item).css("background-color", "pink");
        }
});
```

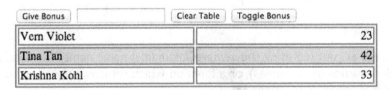

However, you can often achieve the same result using selectors, with better performance.

```
$("tr.manager").css("background-color", "pink");
```

http://jsperf.com/jquery-selector-vs-hasclass

Exercise: Add and toggle styles to modify the display

In this exercise you will enable visual selection of displayed items, and set a persistent display message based on whether a specific class of items are among those selected.

After completion, you should be able to:

- Add and remove classes at runtime

- Test whether an element has been assigned a specified class

Steps

Review project files

1. Open the following project and review its starting HTML and CSS files:

    `/ftjq/4-modify-css`

2. Notice the files are identical to the completed state of the prior exercise.

Create and style a hidden message block

3. In *index.html*, as the bottom of the *#controlBar div*, add a *span* with the phrase *You've got a deal!*, with the *span id* assigned as *saleMessage*.

```
<div id="controlBar">
    <select id="categories">
        <option value="all">All</option>
        <option value="office">Office</option>
        <option value="home">Home</option>
        <option value="sale">Sale</option>
    </select>
    <span id="saleMessage">You've got a deal!</span>
</div>
```

4. In *css/style.css*, add a *.selected class* which sets the *background-color* to *#04c283*.

```
.selected {
    background-color: #04c283;
}
```

5. Add an *id* rule for *#saleMessage* with the following properties. Note that the *#saleMessage div* will be initially invisible due to the *display* property.

```
#saleMessage {
    font: italic bold 14px, sans-serif;
    color: #cf4d47;
    border: 5px solid red;
    padding: 5px;
    display: none;
}
```

Toggle style on selected items

6. In *js/script.js*, add a *click* event handler for all *div* elements with the class *.item*.

7. When items are clicked, toggle the *.selected* class on this *.item*.

8. Your code should look like this:

```
$(".item").on("click", function() {
    $(this).toggleClass("selected");
});
```

9. Save your changes and browse *index.html*. The background color should change when you click on an item, and change back on a second click.

 Glitter are only $0.95

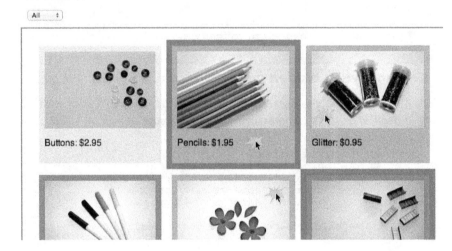

Conditionally display message based on class of selected items

10. In *js/script.js*, in the *click* hander written above, write a condition testing whether any currently selected *.item* also has the *sale* class.

11. If so, set the *display* property of *#saleMessage* to *inline*, otherwise set its *display* to *none*.

12. Your code should look like this:

```
// toggle background when item is clicked
$(".item").on("click", function() {
    $(this).toggleClass("selected");
    // if any selected item is on sale, display sale message, else hide
    if ($(".item.selected").hasClass("sale")) {
        $("#saleMessage").css("display", "inline");
    } else {
        $("#saleMessage").css("display", "none");
    }
});
```

13. Save your changes and browse *index.html*. Select items. If any selected item is on sale, the sale message should appear. It will disappear if all sale items are unselected.

14. Close all project files.

Summary

In this unit you have learned:

- jQuery 1.6+ refers element attributes as *properties*.

- Element properties are modified using the *.prop(name, value)* method.

- Custom data may be assigned to an object using the *.data(name, value)* method.

- Data may also be assigned using a constructor, as *.data(new Item(val1, val2))*.

- jQuery tracks element data using a unique key added to the element as an attribute.

- The child Text node of an element can be modified using the *.text()* method.

- Child HTML nodes and text can be replaced using the *.html()* method.

- Styles may be added using *.css()* or *.addClass()*

- Classes may be removed with *.removeClass()* and tested with *.hasClass()*

- Classes may be toggled using *.toggleClass()*

Review

1. How could you modify an anchor target based on browser data?

2. How could you change the size of an image when it is clicked?

3. You want to change one word in a paragraph in response to a user event. How could you make this happen?

4. You are displaying a calendar date in a *div* with id *#date*. How could you store a set of appointment names and times for that date, for display only when the *#date* is clicked?

5. Can you modify a *div* to display an *h2* element? How?

6. What is the best way to set a style on all table rows assigned the class *manager*? What is another way to do this? When might you use each approach?

Unit 5
Making content and data requests

Objectives

After completing this unit, you should understand:

- How jQuery simplifies using the JavaScript *XMLHttpRequest* object

- Loading selected content from an external page to selected elements in the page

- Writing, requesting, loading, and using JSON data

- Sending parameters with remote data requests

- Handling the full lifecycle of request related events

Loading external content into the page

Loading a document to a selected target

The *jQuery .load(url)* method replaces the child content of selected elements with content specified by a URL.

```
<div id="inventory"></div>
...
// update inventory report every 30 seconds by replacing
// elements inside the #inventory div with new elements
setInterval(function() {
        $("#inventory").load("inventory_report.html");
}, 30000);
```

Loading a specific element to a selected target

Selecting a specific element to load

One or more jQuery selectors may be added to the URL in *.load(url)*, to specify particular element(s) in the loaded document to overwrite content in the target element(s).

```
<div id="inventory">
        <div id="staples"></div>
</div>
...
// update item inventory report
$("#inventory #staples").load("inventory_report.html #staples_count");
```

Note, a space is <u>required</u> between the URL and selector, else the URL may be interpreted by browsers as referring to a URL fragment.

Dynamically specifying the element to load

The selector is simply part of the string URL, so it may be generated dynamically.

```
$("#itemSelector").change(function() {
    ...
    // load full static inventory_report.html, but display selected element
    $("#itemInventory").load("inventory_report.html #" + $(this).val());
});
```

Parameterizing and handling .load() requests

Specifying a callback function in the .load() method

An optional second argument may be used to specify a function to be called immediately after the *.load()* method has successfully requested its content, and prior to it being displayed.

```
$("#itemSelector").change(function() {
    ...
    // get currently selected item in #itemSelector
    var selectedItem = $(this).val();

    // FILTER CONTENT ON CLIENT
    // load full static inventory_report.html, but select for one item,
    // then execute callback

    $("#itemInventory").load("inventory_report.html #" + selectedItem,
        markReported(selectedItem));
});

function markReported(selectedItem) {
    $("#" + selectedItem).css("font-weight", "bold");
}
```

Passing URL parameters via the .load() method

The *.load()* method makes no distinction between requesting static HTML files, and requesting HTML generated dynamically by whatever method (CFML, PHP, JSP, ASPX, etc.)

URL parameters may be specified as additional *.load()* method arguments as *name=value* pairs. A callback function specified as the last argument will still also be called.

```
$("#itemSelector").change(function() {
    ...
    // get currently selected item in #itemSelector
    var selectedItem = $(this).val();

    // FILTER CONTENT ON SERVER
    // load and display selected item from dynamic inventory_report.php
    $("#itemInventory").load("inventory_report.php", "item=" + selectedItem,
        markReported(selectedItem));

    // Note, may also write URL parameters directly onto the URL
    // $("#itemInventory").load("inventory_report.php?item=" + selectedItem,
        markReported(selectedItem));

});
```

Exercise: Loading external content

In this exercise you will load and display an external inventory report in a targeted element of the current page. You will then generate a selector load only a user-determined section of the external report.

After completion, you should be able to:

- Load external content to a targeted element

- Select specific external page content to load

- Trigger a specified event on a selected element

- Invoke a callback function after external content loads

Steps

Review project files

1. Open the following project and review its starting files, including *inventory_report.html*.

   `/ftjq/5-load-content`

2. Specifically notice the new *id* values associated with its various *div* and *span* elements, both in *index.html* and *inventory_report.html*.

   - *div ids:* itemSelector, itemInventory, inventory

   - *span ids:* in-stock, on-order

3. Browse *index.html*, and notice the newly added *#itemSelector* control.

Note, the jQuery.load() method used in this exercise loads content via an XMLHttpRequest object. *This exercise may not work correctly in all browsers if pages are browsed from the file system.* Please follow the Setup Guide instructions to ensure you are loading and browsing pages from a local HTTP server. Optional steps require that this HTTP server be configured to process and render PHP scripts.

Load external page and display in targeted element

4. In *js/script.js*, add a *change* event handler for the *#itemSelector* control.

5. In the event handler, *.load()* *inventory_report.html* into the *#itemInventory* element.

```
$("#itemSelector").change(function() {
    $("#itemInventory").load("inventory_report.html");
});
```

6. Save your changes and browse *index.html*. Change the select control, and you should see the full inventory report loaded into the *#itemInventory div* element.

 Pencils are only $~~$1.95~~ $1.56

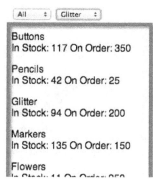

Load and display specified elements in target

7. In *js/script.js*, modify the *.load()* method to add a #pencils selector to the URL. Be sure there is a space between the URL and the selector.

```
$("#itemSelector").change(function() {
    $("#itemInventory").load("inventory_report.html #pencils");
});
```

8. Save your changes, and browse the page. Change the select control, and you should see only the Pencils inventory (regardless of the item selected).

 Glitter are only $0.95

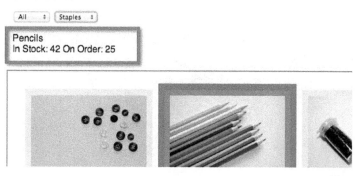

9. In *js/script.js*, replace *"pencils"* with the current *.val()* of this select control, concatenated to the hash ("#") symbol, to dynamically generate the selector.

```
$("#itemSelector").change(function() {
    $("#itemInventory").load("inventory_report.html #" + $(this).val());

});
```

10. Save your changes and browse the page. Select an item to view its inventory data.

11. In *js/script.js*, add a second selector to the *.load()* method, so that only *.in-stock* inventory is displayed.

Note, .in-stock is a class selector, not id selector, but still requires a space between it and the prior selector. This is slightly different than how selectors are chained when used in the jQuery function itself.

```
$("#itemSelector").change(function() {
    $("#itemInventory").load("inventory_report.html #"
        + $(this).val() + " .in-stock");
});
```

12. Save your changes and browse the page. Select an item to view its inventory data, and notice only the *.in-stock* portion of the report for this item is now displayed.

Trigger an event on a selected element

13. In *js/script.js*, remove the *.in-stock* selector added in the previous step.

14. After the *$("#itemSelector").change(...)* event handler, *.trigger()* a *change* event on *#itemSelector*, so inventory data is loaded at startup for the default item in the selector.

```
$("#itemSelector").change(function() {
      $("#itemInventory").load("inventory_report.html #" + $(this).val());
});
$("#itemSelector").trigger("change");
```

15. Save your changes and browse the page. You should see the *#buttons* inventory is initially loaded, as Button is the default option in the *#itemSelector* control.

Invoke a callback function after external content has loaded

16. In *js/script.js*, declare a function named *markReported* with an argument *selectedItem*.

17. In this function, use *selectedItem* to create an ID selector to select that item on the page, and use the *.css(style, value)* method to change its *font-weight* style to *bold*.

18. Your code should look like this:

```
function markReported(selectedItem) {
      $("#" + selectedItem).css("font-weight", "bold");
}
```

19. In the *$("#itemSelector").change(...)* event handler, modify your code so that the *.val()* of this selected item is assigned to a local *var selectedItem*.

20. Modify your code to use *selectedItem* in the *.load()* method, in place of *$(this).val()*.

21. Add a second argument to the *.load()* method, calling your *markReported()* function and passing *selectedItem* as its argument.

22. Your code should look like this:

```
$("#itemSelector").change(function() {
      var selectedItem = $(this).val();
      $("#itemInventory").load("inventory_report.html #"
            + selectedItem, markReported(selectedItem));
});
$("#itemSelector").trigger("change");

function markReported(selectedItem) {
      $("#" + selectedItem).css("font-weight", "bold");
}
```

23. Save your changes and browse the page. Once an item has had its inventory displayed, its name and price should change to bold.

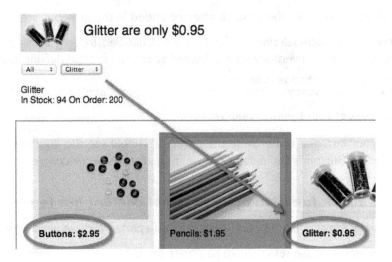

Load and use dynamically generated content

24. Using a web browser, browse the *inventory_report.php* script in the */ftjq/5-load-external* project. You should see rendered output identical to *inventory_report.html*.

```
http://localhost:[port]/ftjq/5-load-external/inventory_report.php
```

25. Add a URL parameter *item=buttons* to the URL, and browse again. You should see a report for only this specified item.

```
http://localhost:[port]/ftjq/5-load-external/inventory_report.php?item=buttons
```

26. In *js/script.js*, in the *$("#itemSelector").change(...)* handler, modify the *.load()* method to request *inventory_report.php*, with the *selectedItem* appended as a URL parameter named *item*, instead of filtering for the selected item on the client as shown above.

```
$("#itemInventory").load("inventory_report.php", "item=" + selectedItem,
    markReported(selectedItem));
```

27. Save your changes and browse the page. You should see no apparent difference, but the inventory data is now being filtered on the server, rather than on the client.

28. Discuss the relative merits of client vs. server side data filtering with the instructor.

29. Close all project files.

Introducing jQuery remote data access

Understanding "Ajax"

The term "Ajax" historically refers to using the browser's *XMLHttpRequest* API to make "Asynchronous JavaScript and XML" requests. In practice, the term now refers to any use of this API to make web server requests for any content or data.

The *XMLHttpRequest* object is widely available across major web browsers. jQuery abstracts away remaining inconsistencies for the functionality it exposes.

Describing the request process

The *XMLHttpRequest* object makes HTTP or HTTPS requests using a supported HTTP request method. HTTP methods (also referred to as "verbs") include:

- *GET* - intended for requests which retrieve a data item, with no other effect
- *POST* - intended for requests which add a new data item

Additional HTTP methods - coming into more common use in support of *Representational State Transfer (REST or "REST-ful")* APIs - are:

- *PUT* - intended for requests which change an existing data item
- *DELETE* - intended for requests which remove an existing data item

Describing the transfer formats

jQuery's AJAX functionality supports several formats for its content or data transfers:

- *text* - unformatted strings
- *html* - text with HTML markup for semantics and/or layout
- *script* - remote JavaScript code
- *json* - data formatted using lightweight JavaScript object and array notation
- *jsonp* - JSON formatted to enable cross-domain requests
- *xml* - data formatted with an arbitrary or defined XML schema

Understanding JSON

JavaScript Object Notation (JSON) is an open standard for describing data structures using combinations of simple arrays and objects. While it originated in JavaScript syntax, parsers are available for all major programming languages.

The JSON standard is described in IETF RFC 4627. It has a recognized internet media type of *application/json*, and standard file extension *.json*.

http://www.json.org/

Formatting data in JSON

JSON is comprised of two basic data structures:

- collection of name/value pairs (commonly called an "object")

- ordered list of values (commonly called an "array")

These structures are combined as needed to represent data sets. The bracket and brace conventions used are common to many languages beyond JavaScript (C, C++, C#, Java, Perl, Python, and others).

Object

```
{
        "name": "Fred",
        "age": 42,
        "address":
                {
                        "street": "123 Fourth St.",
                        "city": "Washington",
                        "province": "D.C."
                }
        "colors": ["red", "green", "blue"]
}
```

Array of Objects

```
[
        {
                "product" : "Buttons",
                "price" : "2.95",
                "image" : "buttons.jpg"
        },
        {
                "product" : "Flowers",
                "price" : "4.95",
                "image" : "flowers.jpg"
        }
]
```

Structures and values are nested as needed to represent the data structure required.

Debating JSON vs XML

JSON is simple and fast. XML supports enforceable schemas and overlapping namespaces. Further discussion points to inform decisions can be found here:

http://blog.technologyofcontent.com/2010/01/json-vs-xml/

http://digitalbazaar.com/2010/11/22/json-vs-xml/

http://stackoverflow.com/search?q=json+vs+xml

http://developer.yahoo.com/javascript/json.html#xml

Loading remote data into the page

Getting and parsing JSON data

Using jQuery.getJSON()

The *$.getJSON(url, callback)* method requests a URL, and invokes a specified callback function after automatically parsing its result as JSON formatted data.

The callback function receives two arguments. The first contains the parsed JSON data. The second contains a status code about the request.

```
$.getJSON("data/products.php", function(data, status) {
      console.log(status, data);
      loadItems(data);
});
```

JSON strings may also be parsed explicitly using *$.parseJSON(json)*.

Understanding callback status codes

All jQuery remote access methods rely on a single underlying *$.ajax()* method, which dispatches the following status codes.

- *success* - request completed normally

- *notmodified* - server returned *304 Not Modified* response

- *error* - request did not complete normally

- *timeout* - request timeout value was exceeded

- *parsererror* - jQuery could not parse the returned value

Event handling related to these status codes is discussed later in this unit.

Using parsed JSON data

Understanding the parsed data

Once parsed by jQuery, JSON data is available as nested JavaScript arrays and objects, as specified by the source JSON.

The following would be parsed as a collection (array) of two objects.

```
[
      {"product" : "Buttons", "price" : "2.95", "image" : "buttons.jpg" },
      {"product" : "Pencils", "price" : "1.95", "image" : "pencils.jpg" }
]
```

The following would be parsed as a JavaScript object with two properties, one holding an array.

```
{
      "SKUcount" : "6",
      "categories" : ["home", "office"]
}
```

Looping over data collections

The jQuery .*each(data, callback)* utility function may be used to loop over a parsed collection (array) of objects. In the .*each()* callback function, each *item* and its *index* are passed as arguments.

The parsed values are used as relevant, such as to create and configure new page elements.

```
[
        {"product" : "Buttons", "price" : "2.95", "image" : "buttons.jpg" },
        {"product" : "Pencils", "price" : "1.95", "image" : "pencils.jpg" }
]
...
$.getJSON("data/products.php", function(data, status) {
     loadItems(data);
});
function loadItems(data) {
     var $div;
     $.each(data, function(index, item) {
            ...
     }
}
```

Comparing $.each() and other loop types

A jQuery $.*each()* loop runs more slowly than a simple JavaScript for loop.

http://jsperf.com/jquery-each-vs-for-loop

However, this is because $.*each()* creates a new function scope for each iteration. This feature protects objects <u>created</u> within the loop, and problems can arise without this scope protection. However, if a loop is only <u>reading</u> data, not creating new objects, you may gain performance by using a JavaScript loop (*for, do, do-while*, etc.) in place of using $.*each()*.

Introducing page element creation

jQuery may be used to create and add new elements as well as select and configure existing elements. Some core techniques are introduced here, and discussed further later in this course.

Creating and configuring a new page element

To create a new page element, pass the element as a string - <u>including its brackets</u> - to the jQuery function. Recall that, by convention, variables assigned jQuery objects begin with $.

```
// create new img, then assign its src

$img = $("<img>");
$img.prop("src", "images/buttons.jpg");

// create a new div and assign its ID, in a chained operation
// using parsed JSON data

function loadItems(data) {
     var $div;
     $.each(data, function(index, item) {
            $div = $("<div>").prop("id", item.product.toLowerCase());
     }
}
```

Understanding creation vs. selection

If you do not include brackets, you <u>select</u> existing elements instead of creating a new one.

```javascript
// create a new img element, configure its src, and assign the new element
// to the $img variable

$img = $("<img>").prop("src", "images/pencils.jpg");

// select all img elements, update their src, and assign the resulting
// collection of images to the $img variable

$img = $("img").prop("src", "images/pencils.jpg");
```

Appending page elements

New elements can be appended to a selected element using the *.append()* method.

```javascript
// add newly configured child element to their parent
// then append the parent to a selected container div

function loadItems(data) {
    var $div;
    $.each(data, function(index, item) {
        $div = $("<div>").prop("id", item.product.toLowerCase());
        $img = $("<img>").prop("src", "images/" + item.image);
        $p = $("<p>").text(item.product + ": $" + item.price);

        $div.append($img).append($p);
        $(".items").append($div);
    }
}
```

Exercise: Loading and configuring elements with JSON data

In this exercise you will use external data to dynamically populate a *select* control, dynamically generate and configure *div* elements to display each data item.

After completion, you should be able to:

- Load remote JSON data and check the result status of the request

- Loop over JSON data to create new elements

- Configure element properties, styles, and data using JSON data

- Assign event handlers to newly created elements

Steps

Review project files

1. Open the following project and review its starting files.

   `/ftjq/5-load-json`

2. In *index.html*, notice the *#itemSelector* options and item divs have been removed.

3. In *data/products.json*, notice the item properties now available: *product, price, image, department, status, inventory, discount.*

Load JSON data and execute callback function

4. In *js/script.js*, use the jQuery *.getJSON()* function to load *data/products.json*, and then call an inline callback function, passing to it two arguments: *data* and *result.*

5. In the callback function, write the *status* and *data* values returned to *console.log().*

   ```
   $.getJSON("data/products.json", function(data, status) {
         console.log(data, status);
   });
   ```

6. Save your changes and browse the page. Open your browser console, and you should see the data contained in *data/products.json*, rendered as an array of JavaScript objects.

```
  ◯  ⬚ Elements  ⬚ Resources  ◉ Network  ⬚ Sources  ◷ Timeline  ⬚ Profile
  success   [Object, Object, Object, Object, Object, Object]
            ▼ 0: Object
                department: "home"
                discount: ".15"
                image: "buttons.jpg"
                inventory: "117"
                price: "2.95"
                product: "Buttons"
                status: "full-price"
              ▶ __proto__: Object
            ▼ 1: Object
                department: "office"
                discount: ".20"
                image: "pencils.jpg"
                inventory: "42"
                price: "1.95"
                product: "Pencils"
                status: "sale"
              ▶ __proto__: Object
            ▶ 2: Object
            ▶ 3: Object
            ▶ 4: Object
            ▶ 5: Object
              length: 6
            ▶ __proto__: Array[0]
  > |
```

Note, the jQuery.getJSON() method used in this exercise loads content via an XMLHttpRequest object. This exercise may not work correctly in all browsers if pages are browsed from the file system. Please follow the Setup Guide to ensure you are loading and browsing through a local HTTP server.

7. Declare two functions named *loadItemSelector* and *loadItems*, passing each an argument named *data*.

8. Call these functions in the *.getJSON()* callback function, passing them its *data* argument.

9. Your code should look like this:

```
$.getJSON("data/products.json", function(data, status) {
    console.log(status, data);
    loadItemSelector(data);
    loadItems(data);
});
function loadItemSelector(data) {

}
function loadItems(data) {

}
```

Create and configure select options using loaded data

10. In the *loadItemSelector()* function, declare a local *var $option*.

11. Use the jQuery *.each()* function to loop over the data and expose each *item* and *index*.

12. Your code should look like this:

```
function loadItemSelector(data) {
    var $option;
    $.each(data, function(index, item) {

    });
}
```

13. In the loop, use the jQuery function to create a new *option* element, and use the *.prop()* method of its jQuery object to configure it with a *value* property ("attribute"), with the lower-cased product name of each *item* as its value. Assign the resulting element to the *$option* variable.

14. Assign *item.product* as *.text()* for this *$option* element.

15. Select the *#itemSelector* element, and *.append()* to it the newly configured *$option*.

16. Your code should look like this:

```
function loadItemSelector(data) {
    var $option;
    $.each(data, function(index, item) {
        $option = $("<option>").prop("value", item.product.toLowerCase());
        $option.text(item.product);
        $("#itemSelector").append($option);
    });
}
```

17. Save your changes and browse the page. You should see the *#itemSelector* populated with each product name in *data/products.json*.

Create and configure item div elements

18. Review the structure of the *#items* and *#item div* elements which were hardcoded into *index.html* in previous exercise. The following step recreate the individual item *div* elements using jQuery.

```
<div id="items" class="display">
  <div id="buttons" class="item home">
    <img src="images/buttons.jpg" width="200" />
    <p><span id="name">Buttons</span>: <span id="price">$2.95</span></p>
  </div>
  <div id="pencils" class="item office sale">
    <img src="images/pencils.jpg" width="200" />
    <p><span id="name">Pencils</span>: <span id="price">$1.95</span></p>
  </div>
  . . .
```

Note, the span tags will not be added in this exercise. They are no longer helpful, because the name and price data they identify in the visual markup is now available in the externally loaded data.

19. In *js/script.js*, in the *loadItem()* function, declare a local *var $div*.

20. Use the jQuery *.each()* function to loop over the data and expose each *item* and *index*.

21. In the loop, assign *$div* a newly created *div* element, configured with the lower-cased product name of each *item* as the value of its *id* property.

22. Your code should look like this:

```
function loadItems(data) {
     var $div;
     $.each(data, function(index, item) {
          $div = $("<div>").prop("id", item.product.toLowerCase());

     });
}
```

23. In a single chained statement, add to *$div* a CSS class of *"item"*, as well as classes named for the *.department* and the *.status* of the current *item*.

24. Assign the entire current *item* object as *.data()* for *$div*.

25. Select the *#items div* and *.append()* this *$div* to it.

26. Your code should look like this:

```
function loadItems(data) {
  var $div;
  $.each(data, function(index, item) {
    $div = $("<div>").prop("id", item.product.toLowerCase());
    $div.addClass("item").addClass(item.department).addClass(item.status);
    $div.data(item);

    $("#items").append($div);
  });
}
```

Note, recall from the prior unit that .data() assigned to an element does not directly affect its markup. Instead, a unique ID is added to the element at runtime, keyed to the jQuery.cache variable.

27. Save your changes and browse the page. You should see the empty, though styled, *div* elements for each item appear in the *#items div*.

28. In *js/script.js*, prior to the *.append()* statement, assign to a new var *$img* a new *img* element, and use *item.image* to assign it a *src* property prepended with the *"images/"* folder name. Also assign it a *width* of 200.

29. Assign to a new var *$p* a new *p* element, and assign *item.product* and *item.price* as its text, separated with a colon and a dollar sign for the *price*.

30. Use the *.append()* method of *$div* to add *$img* and *$p* to it.

31. Your code should look like this:

```
function loadItems(data) {
  var $div;
  $.each(data, function(index, item) {
    $div = $("<div>").prop("id", item.product.toLowerCase());
    $div.addClass("item").addClass(item.department).addClass(item.status);
    $div.data(item);
    $img = $("<img>").prop("src", "images/" + item.image).prop("width", 200);
    $p = $("<p>").text(item.product + ": $" + item.price);
    $div.append($img).append($p);

    $("#items").append($div);
  });
}
```

32. Save your changes and browse the page. You should now see configured *div* elements generated from external data, matching the hardcoded elements in previous exercises.

33. In *js/script.js*, prior to the *.append()* statement, use the *.on()* method to assign *$div* a "*mouseover*" event handler, using an inline function.

34. Use the *src* property value of *this img* being moused over to assign the *src* property of the *#image* element at the top of the page.

35. Following this event handler, assign a second "*mouseover*" event handler, but in this case assign the *displayPrice* function (pre-written in *js/script.js*) as its callback.

36. Review the *displayPrice()* function to notice it uses *$(this)* references to access the *.data()* properties of the *item* being moused over, previously set as you configured each *$div*.

37. Your code should look like this:

```
function loadItems(data) {
  var $div;
  $.each(data, function(index, item) {

    ...

    $div.on("mouseover", function() {
      var path = $("img", this).prop("src");
      $("#image").prop("src", path);
    });
    $div.on("mouseover", displayPrice);

    $("#items").append($div);
  });
}
```

38. Save your changes and browse the page. The items should now respond to mouseover events by displaying their *image*, *name*, *price*, and discounted price if on sale.

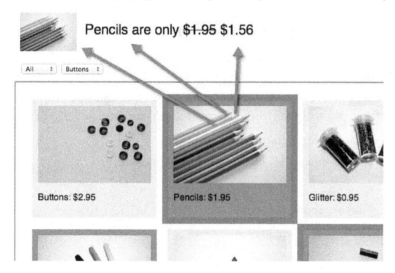

39. Close all project files.

Sending request parameters and handling events

Surveying jQuery's remote access functions

jQuery supports a range of specialized remote access functions. Each of these rely on the underlying $.ajax() function.

$(selector).load(url) - load content into selected element

$.post(url, data, callback) - send a POST request with optional data, then execute callback

$.get(url, data, callback) - send a GET request with optional data, then execute callback

$.getJSON(url, data, callback) - send a GET/POST request with optional data, parse result as JSON, then execute callback

$.getScript(url, callback) - request remove JavaScript file, execute result, then execute callback

Introducing the jQuery.ajax() function

All of jQuery's remote access functionality relies on the *$.ajax(options)* function, which abstracts use of the underlying JavaScript *XMLHttpRequest* object.

Its *options* argument - commonly written inline - supports optional properties to configure its behaviors, such as those already seen using the *.load()* method and *$.getJSON()* function.

For example, the following statements are equivalent.

```
$.getJSON("data/product.json", loadSelectedItem);
...
$.ajax({
        type: "GET",
        url: "data/products.json",
        dataType: "json",
        success: loadSelectedItem
});
```

Surveying the $.ajax() function options

Common Ajax configuration options include the following. A full list can be found here:

http://api.jquery.com/jQuery.ajax/

type - *GET, POST, PUT, DELETE,* or other browser-supported HTTP methods ("verbs")

url - the path to be requested (data appended as parameters, if type is GET)

data - string of *name=value* pairs, or *object* (sent as URL params or headers, based on type)

dataType - *text, html, script, json, jsonp, xml* (parsing is by *content-type* header if left undefined)

contentType - defaults to *application/x-www-form-urlencoded* (override to post documents, etc.)

timeout - milliseconds before a timeout *error* event is dispatched

cache - if set *false*, jQuery alters URL on each request to override browser resource caching

Using $.ajax() for detailed remote script requests

Introducing JSONP

Browsers implement a *same origin policy* by default. Dependent resource requests (such as for images) are blocked if made to domains other than the one which delivered the page. The exception is requests for external script files made from a <script src="URL"></script> block.

JSONP ("JSON with Prefix") is a technique which enables cross-origin JSON requests by modifying a particular request for JSON data by wrapping it as a <script> request which parses the loaded resource - which is JSON - and assigns the resulting data to a specified variable.

jQuery enables this technique with its *jsonp dataType*.

```
$.ajax({
      type: "GET",
      url: "http://www.foo.com/products.php",
      dataType: "jsonp",
      success: loadSelectedItem
});
```

Sending parameters with a request

Data may be assigned as either a string of *name=value* pairs, or as a JavaScript *object*. If set as an object, the *jQuery.param()* utility function is used internally to convert it to a *urlencoded* string.

```
$.ajax({
      type: "GET",
      url: "data/products.php",
      data: {"item": "buttons", "status": "full-price" },
      dataType: "json",
      success: loadSelectedItem
});
```

Handling request timeouts

A request *timeout* may be set in milliseconds, after which a request will dispatch an error event, to be handled by an assigned error event handler.

```
function requestData() {
      $.ajax({
            type: "GET",
            url: "data/products.php",
            data: {"item": "buttons", "status": "full-price" },
            dataType: "json",
            success: loadSelectedItem,
            timeout: 3000,
            error: errorHandler
      });
}
```

Error handlers receive the *XHLHttpRequest*, *status*, and *error* object (varies based on the error).

```
function errorHandler(xhr, status, error) {
      console.log(status); // logs "timeout" if timeout exceeded
      // try a limited number of repeat requests
      if (status === "timeout") {
            timeoutCount++;
            if (timeoutCount < 3) requestData();
      }
}
```

Handling the request life cycle

The *$.ajax()* method executes multiple event callbacks for each request, including:

beforeSend - called before request, and is passed the *XMLHttpRequest* ("XHR") and *options* objects as arguments. Can return *false* in this function to abort the request.

```
function beforeSendHandler(xhr, options) { ... }
```

success - called if request returns without error, passed *data*, *status*, and *XHR* object

```
function successHandler(data, status, xhr) { ... }
```

error - called if request has an error, and is passed the *XHR*, *status*, and *error* objects

```
function errorHandler(xhr, status, error) { ... }
```

complete - called after <u>either</u> a *success* or *error* result, and is passed the *XHR* and *status* objects

```
function completeHandler(xhr, status) { ... }
```

Exercise: Using Ajax parameters and callbacks

In this exercise you will will configure the lower-level *$.ajax()* function to make a parameterized request for product data from a remote PHP script, and handle its beforeSend, success, complete, and error events.

After completion, you should be able to:

- Request remote resources using *$.ajax()*

- Configure and send a *data* object with a request

- Handle *success*, *beforeSend*, and *complete* events

- Handle request timeout and 404 file not found errors

Steps

Review project files

1. Open the following project and review its starting files.

    `/ftjq/5-ajax-params-callbacks`

2. In *js/script.js*, notice

    - *#itemSelector change* event handler, which assigns the currently selected *option* value to a local *var selectedItem*.

    - Near line 63, the *$.getJSON()* request built previously now requests the *data/products.php* script and not the static *data/products.json* file.

    - Four pre-built functions: *loadSelectedItem, beforeSendHandler, errorHandler, completeHandler*

3. Open *data/products.php*, notice the product data is now generated, and that a GET URL parameter named *item* may be passed to filter the returned data to a specified item.

Request filtered data using a $.ajax() request

4. In *js/script.js*, in the *#itemSelector change* event handler, declare a local *var filter* and assign it an empty inline object.

5. Write a condition testing *if selectedItem* is not *"all"*.

6. If the condition is *true*, assign *filter* an inline object with a property *item* with the *selectedItem* variable as its value.

7. Your code should look like this:

```
$("#itemSelector").change(function() {
      var selectedItem = $(this).val();
      var filter = {};
      if (selectedItem != "all") {
            filter = { "item" : selectedItem };
      }

});
```

8. Write a request using the $.ajax() function, with the following properties assigned to an inline object being passed to this function:

- *type:* "GET"

- *url:* "data/products.php"

- *data:* filter

- *dataType:* "json"

- *success:* loadSelectedItem

9. Your code should look like this:

```
var filter = {};
if (selectedItem != "all") {
        filter = { "item" : selectedItem };
}

$.ajax({
        type: "GET",
        url: "data/products.php",
        data: filter,
        dataType: "json",
        success: loadSelectedItem
});
```

10. Save your changes and request the page. Select an item in *#itemSelector*, and the display should update to show only that item.

© 2013 Fig Leaf Software, Inc.

Implement beforeSend and complete event handlers

11. In *js/script.js*, in the *$.ajax()* function, assign *beforeSendHandler* and *completeHandler* to their corresponding events.

```
$.ajax({
        type: "GET",
        url: "data/products.php",
        data: filter,
        dataType: "json",
        success: loadSelectedItem,
        beforeSend: beforeSendHandler,
        complete: completeHandler
});
```

12. Save your changes and browse the page, with the JavaScript console open. Select an item, and examine the console output.

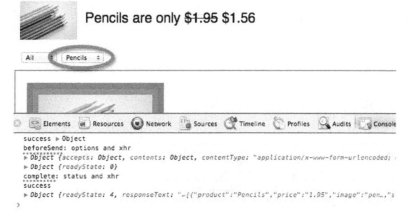

Handle a data request timeout

13. In *data/products.php*, near Line 19, uncomment the *sleep(5)* function. This will create a 5 second delay when calling this script.

```
...
// delay response 5 seconds to explore jQuery ajax request timeout handling
sleep(5);

$selected_item = $_GET["item"];
...
```

14. In *js/script.js*, assign a *3000* millisecond *timeout* in the *$.ajax()* function.

15. Assign *errorHandler* to handle *error* events dispatched by the *$.ajax()* function.

16. Your code should look like this:

```
$.ajax({
        type: "GET",
        url: "data/products.php",
        data: filter,
        dataType: "json",
        timeout: 3000,
        success: loadSelectedItem,
        beforeSend: beforeSendHandler,
        complete: completeHandler,
        error: errorHandler
});
```

17. Save your changes and request the page, with the JavaScript console open. You should notice a 5 second delay before items initially load. Select an item. You should see beforeSend log information, then a 3 second delay followed by a timeout error.

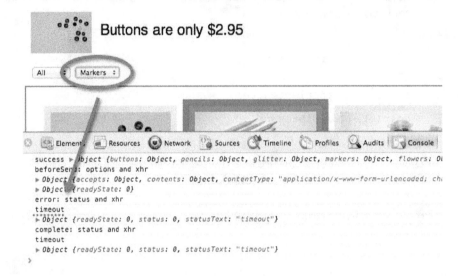

Handle a 404 file not found error

18. In *js/script.js*, remove the letter "s" in the *url* of *data/products.php* in the *$.ajax()* function.

19. Modify the *errorHandler* function by adding a third argument *error*, and logging its value.

```
function errorHandler(xhr, status, error) {
    console.log("error: status and xhr");
    console.log(status);
    console.log(error);
    console.log(xhr);
}
```

20. Save your changes and requst the page with the JavaScript console open. The page should load correctly, as the initial data is loaded by the correct path. Select an item, and you should see the 404 error output to the console.

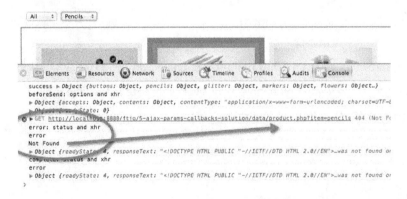

21. Close all project files.

Summary

In this unit you have learned:

- jQuery supports remote requests using the $.ajax() function

- The $.ajax() function abstracts the JavaScript *XMLHttpRequest* object

- Several higher level functions are available to simplify using $.ajax()
    - $(selector).load(url)
    - $.get(url, data, callback)
    - $.post(url, data, callback)
    - $.getJSON(url, data, callback)
    - $.getScript(url, callback)

- $(selector).load(url) loads all or selected elements of an external page

- JSON data relies on JavaScript object and array notation to define data structures

- $.getJSON(url, data, callback) method parses its JSON results into data for its callback

- $.each(data, function(index, item) { ... }) can be used to loop over JSON results

- New page elements are created by passing <u>tags</u> to the jQuery function: $("<img>")

- $.ajax(options) can be configured to support:
    - any HTTP method
    - data parameters
    - various return dataTypes
    - various posted contentTypes
    - request timeouts
    - browser caching override
    - request lifecycle events: beforeSend, success, error, complete
    - additional options ...

Review

1. You want to abort a request if a browser is offline. How could you approach this?

2. You want to load divs of a specific class - only - from an external page. How?

3. Your JSON request returns an array of objects providing image names and paths. How would you display them all?

4. Regardless whether a data request succeeds, you must disable a button. How?

5. You must pass three named parameters to a PHP script. How?

Unit 6
Modifying page structure without reload

Objectives

After completing this unit, you should understand:

- Why there is no need to load another page if the current one has the data
- How newly created or existing page elements can be
  - appended or prepended
  - inserted before or after
  - selected in relation as parent, child, or sibling
  - detached, removed, or emptied
  - cloned with or without data and events
  - wrapped with new markup
- How event handlers can be assigned to both existing and later-created elements

Introducing page structure modification

Understanding the need

Historically, pages layout changes in response to a script request (PHP, CFML, ASP, JSP, etc.). But, why request a new page if the information already in the browser?

When would any of these scenarios require a server request? When wouldn't they? Remember, jQuery can store "hidden" element data.

- display selected item detail
- move selected items to a different area ("shopping cart")
- sort listed items between one another
- create new display for selected items
- delete items from a list

Note, this unit covers many key aspects of the page modification API, but does not attempt to show all available methods, approaches, or optional parameters. JQuery documentation is available here:

http://api.jquery.com/

Creating and using new page elements

Creating new elements from input or JSON data

Creating new elements

As already seen, new elements are created by passing markup to the jQuery function.

```
$paragraph = $("<p/>");
$table = $("<table><tr><th>Name</th><th>Address</th></tr></table>");
```

Attributes can be set by markup, or by a properties object passed as a second argument.

```
// configure attributes while creating jQuery object for the element
$div = $("<div id='items' class='container' />");

// or, configure attributes using a separate configuration object $img = $
("<img/>", {src: "images/item1.jpg, alt: "item"});

// or, separate creation and configuration
function imgConfig(src, alt) {
        this.src = src;
        this.alt = alt;
}
var config = new imgConfig("images/item1.jpg", "item");
$img = $("<img/>", config);
```

Creating new elements from loaded data

As already seen, we can load and loop over external data. The values would be commonly used to create and append new page elements.

```
$table = $("<table><tr><th>Last Name</th></tr></table>");
$.getJSON("data/people.json", function(data) {
        $.each(data, function(index, item) {
                $row = $("<tr><td>" + item.lastName + "</td></tr>");
                $table.append($row);
        });
});
$("#container").append($table);
```

Last Name
Tourquoise
Brown
Orange
Red
Purple

Varying the creation process

Code being code, there are many ways to reach the same result; particularly in jQuery, which supports long chained statements.

```
$.each(data, function(index, item) {
    // $row = $("<tr><td>" + item.lastName + "</td></tr>");
    $row = $("<tr/>").append("<td/>").text(item.lastName);
    $table.append($row);
});
```

Chained methods operate on the <u>initial</u> object in the chained statement.

Which approach is "better" is debatable, and varies greatly by browser and platform. Generally speaking, it's better to create individual elements with jQuery and assemble them. This tends to process faster than passing long HTML strings, or using JavaScript .innerHTML directly.

http://jsperf.com/creating-complex-elements

Adding elements in relation to others

Understanding target vs. content

target - the element to which other elements are being added

content - the elements being added to a target element

jQuery supports common page modification behaviors (appending, prepending, etc.) with two alternate methods, each of which may be easier to use in certain contexts.

	target.method(content)	*content.method(target)*
add as next child	`$target.`**`append`**`($content)`	`$content.`**`appendTo`**`($target)`
add as first child	`$target.`**`prepend`**`($content)`	`$content.`**`prependTo`**`($target)`
insert after target	`$target.`**`after`**`($content)`	`$content.`**`insertAfter`**`($target)`
insert before target	`$target.`**`before`**`($content)`	`$content.`**`insertBefore`**`($target)`

Appending and prepending content

Elements are added as the <u>next</u> child using *target.append(element)* or *element.appendTo(target)*.

```
$row = $("<tr/>").append("<td/>").text("Orange").css("font-weight", "bold");
$("#peopleTable").append($row);
       // or
$row.appendTo("#peopleTable");
```

Indigo
Violet
Orange

Elements are added as a <u>first</u> child using *target.prepend(element)* or *element.prependTo(target)*.

```
$row = $("<tr/>").append("<td/>").text("Orange").css("font-weight", "bold");
$("#peopleTable").prepend($row);
       // or
$row.prependTo("#peopleTable");
```

Orange
Indigo
Violet

Adding content before or after its target

Elements are placed <u>before</u> their target using *target.before(content)* or *content.insertBefore(target)*.

```
<h2 id="teamTitle">Team Members</h2>
...
$("#teamTitle").before("<hr/>");
       // or
$("<hr/>").insertBefore("#teamTitle");
```

Team Members

Elements are added <u>after</u> their target using *target.after(content)* or *target.insertAfter(content)*.

```
<h2 id="teamTitle">Team Members</h2>
...
$("#teamTitle").after("<hr/>");
       // or
$("<hr/>").insertAfter("#teamTitle");
```

Team Members

Assigning event handlers to new elements

Understanding the recently deprecated approaches

Prior to jQuery 1.7, two methods were used for assigning event handlers.

The *.bind(event, function)* method assigns a handler to matching element(s) which already exist.

```
$("#button").bind("click", function(event) { ... });
```

http://api.jquery.com/bind/

The *.live(event, function)* method assigns a handler to matching element(s) which already exist, as well as any elements created later which match the same selector.

```
$(".displayBox").live("mouseover", function(event) { ... });
```

http://api.jquery.com/live/

As of jQuery 1.7, the *.live(event, function)* method is formally deprecated, and the *.on(event, function)* method - described next - is preferred to the *.bind(event, function)* method for dynamic event handler assignment.

Assigning event handlers during element creation

When creating and assembling new elements, the *.on(event, function)* method is used to assign event handlers.

```
$mybutton = $("<button/>").text("Buy");
$mybutton.on("click", function(event) {
        alert("It's yours!");
});
$("#container1").append($mybutton);
```

Events attached with *.on(event, function)* can be removed with *.off(event, selector)*. Event handlers may also be added for one-time only use with *.one(event, function)*.

http://api.jquery.com/on/

Understanding dynamic handler creation

Event handlers assigned using *.on(event, function)* are assigned to <u>each</u> individual element matching the selector through which this method is called. Such as each cell in a table.

```
$("#products td").on("mouseover", function(event) {
        alert(event.target.innerHTML);
});
```

Selecting parents and children of target elements

Understanding the need

The element from which an event is dispatched is often different than the element to be changed in response. For example, you may want to click a button, but move its entire row.

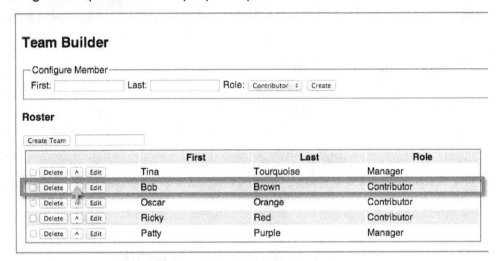

Retrieving nesting and nested elements

jQuery supports methods for accessing page elements in relation to a selected element. They are optionally filtered by a selector so only matching elements are retrieved.

.parent([selector]) - returns the parent (nesting) element, optionally matching a selector

.parents([selector]) - returns all parent (nesting) elements, optionally matching a selector

.children([selector]) - return all child (nested) element, optionally matching a selector

An example would be accessing a table row when an element in that row is clicked.

```
$(".edit").on("click", function(event) {
    $button = $(event.target);
    $cell = $button.parent();
    console.log($cell);
    $table = $button.parents("table");
    console.log($table);
});
```

Removing elements from the page

Elements can be removed, each optionally filtered by a selector so that only matching elements are removed. Text is also removed, as text is considered a child node of an element.

.detach([selector]) - remove the element and its children, but leave related data and event handlers, so they need not be re-created when the elements are restored

.empty([selector]) - remove the children of the element, along with their data and events.

.remove([selector]) - remove the element, its children, and all related data and event handlers

```
$(".edit").on("click", function(event) {
    $button = $(event.target);
    // select table row surrounding button
    $row = $button.parents("tr");
    alert("Removing: \n\n" + $row[0].outerHTML);
    $row.remove();
});
```

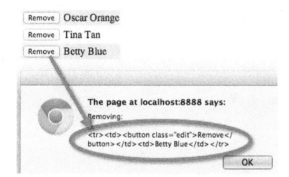

Exercise: Creating, appending, and deleting page elements

In this exercise you will create a form which creates and adds table rows from user input or external data, and enables deletion of any selected row.

After completion, you should be able to:

- Append elements using .append or .appendTo methods

- Create, configure, and append nested page elements

- Assign event handlers which interact with nesting parent elements

- Use external data to load a dynamically generated table

Steps

Review project files

1. Open the following project and review its starting files.

   `/ftjq/6-create-append`

2. In *index.html*, notice these elements

   - *configureMember* form

   - *firstName* and *lastName* text fields

   - *role* select field

   - *rowId* hidden field

   - *configureButton* button element

   - *createTeamButton* button element

   - *teamName* text field

   - *rosterTable* table

   - *tr* with *class* .headerRow, and *First*, *Last*, and *Role* th elements

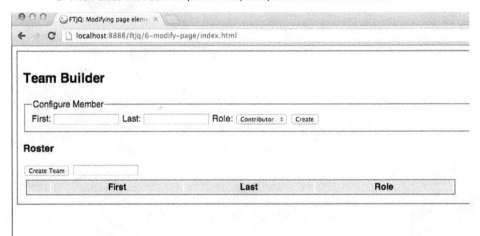

Create and add new table rows

3. In *js/script.js*, review the pre-written code in the *$("#configureButton").click(...)* event handler.

    - call *event.preventDefault()* to prevent *form* submission

      ```
      event.preventDefault();
      ```

    - get *this* button's *text* to indicate *action* to take (*text* will change at runtime)

      ```
      var action = $(this).text();
      ```

    - selected form field *.val()* are assigned to like-named properties of a *formData object*

      ```
      var formData = {};
      formData.firstName = $("input[name='firstName']").val();
      formData.lastName = $("input[name='lastName']").val();
      formData.role = $("select[name='role']").val();
      formData.rowId = $("input[name='rowId']").val();
      ```

4. After the existing code, declare a local *var $row* and assign to it the result of calling the *createRow(item)* function, and passing it the *formData* object.

    ```
    var $row = createRow(formData);
    ```

5. In the pre-built but empty *createRow(item)* function, declare a local *var $row*, and use the jQuery function to assign it a new *tr* element.

6. Declare a local *var $controls* and a assign it a new *td* element with *class controls*.

7. Append the *$controls* element to the *$row*.

8. Your code should look like this:

    ```
    function createRow(item) {

        var $row = $("<tr/>");
        var $controls = $("<td class='controls'/>");
        $row.append($controls);

        . . .
    ```

9. Next, as a single statement, create a new *td* element. Add to it the *firstName class*, and the *item.firstName* field as its *text*. Then *append* this new object to *$row*.

    ```
    $("<td/>").addClass("firstName").text(item.firstName).appendTo($row);
    ```

10. Use copy-paste to repeat this statement twice, modifying it as needed to create *td* elements for the *lastName* and *role* fields.

11. Your code should look like this:

    ```
    function createRow(item) {
        var $row = $("<tr/>");
        var $controls = $("<td class='controls'/>");
        $row.append($controls);

        $("<td/>").addClass("firstName").text(item.firstName).appendTo($row);
        $("<td/>").addClass("lastName").text(item.lastName).appendTo($row);
        $("<td/>").addClass("role").text(item.role).appendTo($row);

        . . .
    ```

12. Review the pre-built *getRowId(baseString)* function, and related global *rowIdCounter* variable, which will create a guaranteed unique value based on a provided base string.

```
var rowIdCounter = 0;
function getRowId(baseString) {
      return (baseString + rowIdCounter++);
}
```

13. In the *createRow(item)* function, after the previous statements assign *$row* an *id* value based on passing *item.lastName* to *getRowId(baseString)*.

14. Return the *$row* from the function.

15. Your complete *createRow(item)* function should look like this:

```
function createRow(item) {

      var $row = $("<tr/>");
      var $controls = $("<td class='controls'/>");
      $row.append($controls);

      $("<td/>").addClass("firstName").text(item.firstName).appendTo($row);
      $("<td/>").addClass("lastName").text(item.lastName).appendTo($row);
      $("<td/>").addClass("role").text(item.role).appendTo($row);

      $row.prop("id", getRowId(item.lastName));
      return $row;
}
```

16. In the *$('#configureButton').click(...)* event handler, below the call to *createRow(item)*, if the *action* is *"Create"* append the new *$row* to *#rosterTable*, then call the pre-built *clearForm()* function.

```
$("#configureButton").click(function(event) {

      ...

      var $row = createRow(formData);
      if(action === "Create") {
            $("#rosterTable").append($row)
            clearForm();
      }

}
```

17. Save your changes and browse *index.html*. You should be able to add new team members to the roster.

© 2013 Fig Leaf Software, Inc.

18. Use your browser developer tools to examine the newly added rows. Notice the *ID* values added to each *tr* element in *#rosterTable*.

```
 ⊗   📑 Elements  📄 Resources  🌐 Network  📋 Sources  ⏱ Timeline  🕐 Profil
▼<html>
  ▶<head>…</head>
  ▼<body>
    ▼<div id="container">
      ▶<div id="messageBar">…</div>
      ▶<div id="controlBar">…</div>
      ▼<div id="rosterContainer">
          <p class="title2">Roster</p>
          <button id="createTeamButton">Create Team</button>
          <input type="text" name="teamName">
        ▼<table id="rosterTable" class="tableDisplay">
          ▼<tbody>
            ▶<tr class="headerRow">…</tr>
          ➤ ▶<tr id="Green0">…</tr>
            ▶<tr id="Kohl1">…</tr>
          </tbody>
        </table>
      </div>
    </div>
    <script type="text/javascript" src="js/jquery-1.8.3.js"></script>
    <script type="text/javascript" src="js/script.js"></script>
```

Remove selected table row

19. In *js/script.js*, in the *createRow(item)* function, above the statement appending *$controls* to *$row*, assign the *$controls* cell (*td* element) the value returned from the pre-built but empty *addDeleteButton($controls)* function.

20. Your code should look like this:

```
function createRow(item) {

    var $row = $("<tr/>");
    var $controls = $("<td class='controls'/>");
    $controls = addDeleteButton($controls);

    $row.append($controls);

    $("<td/>").addClass("firstName").text(item.firstName).appendTo($row);

    ...
```

21. In the *addDeleteButton($controls)* function, create a new *button* element with *Delete* as its *text*, and assign it to a local *var $deleteButton*.

22. Assign a *click* event handler *on $deleteButton*.

23. In the *click* event handler, select the *tr* elements from the *.parents()* of *this* button which dispatched the event, and call the *.remove()* method on this row.

24. Append *$deleteButton* to the *$controls* cell passed into this function, then return the *$controls* cell, which now contains a *button* with a *click* event handler.

25. Your code should look like this:

```
function addDeleteButton($controls) {

    $deleteButton = $("<button>").text("Delete");
    $deleteButton.on("click", function() {
        $(this).parents("tr").remove();
    });
    $deleteButton.appendTo($controls);
    return $controls;
}
```

Note, you could alternately append the button as $controls.append($deleteButton). Which approach is better depends on context. The .appendTo() method is particularly helpful in chained statements.

26. Save your changes and browse *index.html*. Add a new member to the roster. You should now see a Delete button the first column. Clicking this button should remove this row.

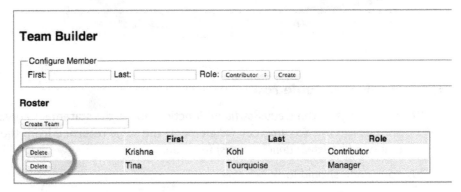

Create and append table rows from external data

27. Open and review *data/people.json*. noticing the field names: *firstName, lastName, role.*

28. In *js/script.js*, above the *createRow(item)* function, use the *$.getJSON()* function to load *data/people.json*, with an anonymous inline event handler receiving a *data* argument.

29. Use the *$.each(index, item)* function to loop over the loaded data.

30. In the loop, as a chained statement, append the result returned by passing the *item* argument to *createRow(item)* to *$row*.

31. Your code should look like this:

```
$.getJSON("data/people.json", function(data) {
    $.each(data, function(index, item) {
        createRow(item).appendTo("#rosterTable");
    });
});

function createRow(item) {

    ...
```

32. Save your changes and browse *index.html*. Because *$.getJSON()* is loading an external file, <u>verify that you are requesting the page through a local HTTP</u> server and not from the file system. You should see the *#rosterTable* populated by the loaded data. Verify that you can add an additional member, and notice where it appends in the table.

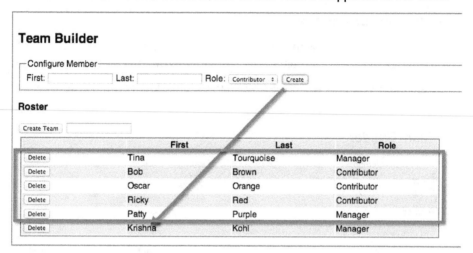

33. Close all project files.

Inserting and replacing elements

Selecting sibling elements

Understanding the need

Users want to interact with content. All page content exists in a hierarchy. So, moving elements within a set of similar elements requires knowing what comes before and after each element.

For example, you may wish to move rows up and down within a table.

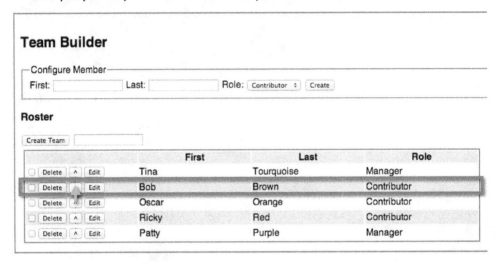

Retrieving sibling elements

jQuery supports methods for accessing sibling elements, all sharing a common parent, such as all table rows in a *table*, or all paragraphs in a common *div*. The methods are optionally filtered by a selector so only matching elements are retrieved.

.prevAll([selector]) - retrieve all preceding siblings as a set

.prev([selector]) - retrieve immediately preceding sibling

.nextAll([selector]) - retrieve all subsequent siblings as a set

.next([selector]) - retrieve next sibling

```
$(".move").on("click", function(event) {
     $button = $(event.target);
     $row = $button.parents("tr");
     $nextRow = $row.next();
     $row.insertAfter($nextRow);
});
```

In addition, *.prevUntil([selector])* and *.nextUntil([selector])* methods are available.

Replacing selected elements

Understanding the need

Pages are visually updated by either changing the properties of a existing elements, or by replacing elements with something new.

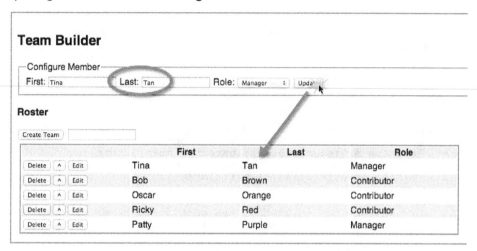

For example, you may replace a table row with a new, updated row.

Replacing page elements

Similar to the appending and insertion methods, jQuery supports two element replacement methods which provide the same behavior, but with alternating target and content.

$(content).replaceAll($target) - use the content to replace all selected targets

$(target).replaceWith($content) - replace all selected targets with the specified content

Replacing page elements example

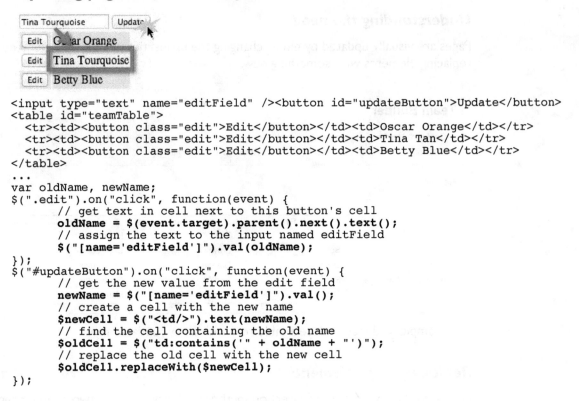

```html
<input type="text" name="editField" /><button id="updateButton">Update</button>
<table id="teamTable">
  <tr><td><button class="edit">Edit</button></td><td>Oscar Orange</td></tr>
  <tr><td><button class="edit">Edit</button></td><td>Tina Tan</td></tr>
  <tr><td><button class="edit">Edit</button></td><td>Betty Blue</td></tr>
</table>
...
var oldName, newName;
$(".edit").on("click", function(event) {
      // get text in cell next to this button's cell
      oldName = $(event.target).parent().next().text();
      // assign the text to the input named editField
      $("[name='editField']").val(oldName);
});
$("#updateButton").on("click", function(event) {
      // get the new value from the edit field
      newName = $("[name='editField']").val();
      // create a cell with the new name
      $newCell = $("<td/>").text(newName);
      // find the cell containing the old name
      $oldCell = $("td:contains('" + oldName + "')");
      // replace the old cell with the new cell
      $oldCell.replaceWith($newCell);
});
```

Exercise: Inserting and replacing elements

In this exercise you will create a button to select and move an element within a group of similar elements. You will also create a button to select elements and copy their values into a form.

After completion, you should be able to:

- Conditionally move similar elements among one another

- Select elements and copy their values into form fields

- Replace all selected elements with a new element

Steps

Review project files

1. Open the following project and review its starting files.

   `/ftjq/6-insert-replace`

2. The files are identical to the completed state of the prior exercise.

Move enclosing parent of selected element

3. In *js/script.js*, in the *createRow(item)* function, below the code adding the *delete* button to *$row*, pass the *$controls* element to the pre-built but empty *addMoveupButton($controls)* function, and assign the result back to *$controls*.

```
function createRow(item) {

        var $row = $("<tr/>");
        var $controls = $("<td class='controls'/>");
        $controls = addDeleteButton($controls);
        $controls = addMoveupButton($controls);

        $row.append($controls);

        ...
```

4. In the *addMoveupButton($controls)* function, create a *button* element with text " ^ " and assign it to local *var $moveupButton*.

5. Assign a click event handler on $moveupButton.

6. Your code should look like this:

```
function addMoveupButton($controls) {
        $moveupButton = $("<button>").text(" ^ ");
        $moveupButton.on("click", function() {

        });
}
```

7. In the *click* event handler, select the row containing the button by selecting the *tr* element from the *.parents()* of *this* button which dispatched the event, and assign it to a local *var $thisRow*.

8. Assign the previous element to *$thisRow* to local *var $previousRow* using *.prev()*.

9. Insert *$thisRow* before *$previousRow* using *.insertBefore()*.

10. Your code should look like this:

```
function addMoveupButton($controls) {
        $moveupButton = $("<button>").text(" ^ ");
        $moveupButton.on("click", function() {
                $thisRow = $(this).parents("tr");
                $previousRow = $thisRow.prev();
                $thisRow.insertBefore($previousRow);
        });
}
```

11. After the event handler, append *$moveupButton* to the *$controls* element, using either the *.append()* or *.appendTo()* syntax.

12. Return *$controls* from the *addMoveupButton($controls)* function.

13. Your code should look like this:

```
function addMoveupButton($controls) {
        $moveupButton = $("<button>").text(" ^ ");
        $moveupButton.on("click", function() {
                $thisRow = $(this).parents("tr");
                $previousRow = $thisRow.prev();
                $thisRow.insertBefore($previousRow);
        });
        $controls.append($moveupButton);
        return $controls;
}
```

14. Save your changes and browse *index.html*. You should be able to move rows up using the *moveupButton*, but they do not stop at the header row.

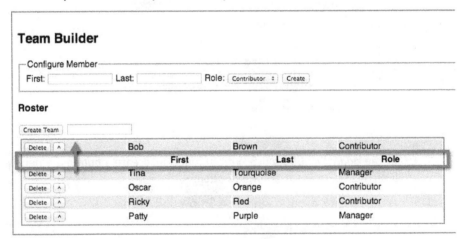

15. In *js/script.js*, surround the statement which inserts *$thisRow* before *$previousRow* in a condition testing if *$previousRow* is <u>not</u> the header row (does not have class *headerRow*).

```
function addMoveupButton($controls) {
        $moveupButton = $("<button>").text(" ^ ");
        $moveupButton.on("click", function() {
                $thisRow = $(this).parents("tr");
                $previousRow = $thisRow.prev();
                if(!($previousRow.hasClass("headerRow"))) {
                        $thisRow.insertBefore($previousRow);
                }
        });
        $controls.append($moveupButton);
        return $controls;
}
```

16. Save your changes and browse *index.html*. You should be able to move rows up, but not above the header row.

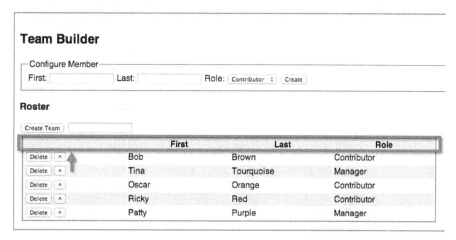

Append button to copy table row data into a form

17. In *js/script.js*, in the *createRow(item)* function, below the code adding the move up button to *$row*, pass the *$controls* element to the pre-built but empty *addEditButton($controls)* function, and assign the result back to *$controls*.

```
function createRow(item) {

        var $row = $("<tr/>");
        var $controls = $("<td class='controls'/>");
        $controls = addDeleteButton($controls);
        $controls = addMoveupButton($controls);
        $controls = addEditButton($controls);

        $row.append($controls);

        ...
```

18. In the *addEditButton($controls)* function, create a *button* element with the text *Edit* and assign it to a local *var $editButton*.

19. Assign the pre-built function named *copyRowToForm()* as a *click* event handler *on $editButton*.

20. Your code should look like this:

```
function addEditButton($controls) {
        $editButton = $("<button>").text("Edit");
        $editButton.on("click", copyRowToForm);

}
```

21. In *index.html*, review the field names and option values in the form.

    • *configureMember* form

    • *firstName* and *lastName* input fields

    • *role* select with Contributor and Manager options

    • *rowId* hidden input

    • *configureButton* button

22. Review the code in *copyRowToForm()*.

    • Selects the *tr* for the table row containing *this* button

        ```
        $row = $(event.target).parents("tr");
        ```

    • Gets the *firstName*, *lastName*, *role*, and *id* values from the row - whether as text or property, as needed - and assign them to like-named local variables.

        ```
        var firstName = $row.find(".firstName").text();
        var lastName = $row.find(".lastName").text();
        var role = $row.find(".role").text();
        var rowId = $row.prop("id");
        ```

    • Selects each corresponding form field by *name* and sets its *.val()*

        ```
        $("[name='firstName']").val(firstName);
        $("[name='lastName']").val(lastName);
        $("[name='role']").val(role);
        $("[name='rowId']").val(rowId);
        ```

    • Finds the button in the form and changes its *text* to *Update*

        ```
        $("#configureMember").find("button").text("Update");
        ```

23. In *addEditButton($controls)* function, return the *$controls* with the *$editButton* appended.

24. Your complete function should look like this:

```
function addEditButton($controls) {
        $editButton = $("<button>").text("Edit");
        $editButton.on("click", copyRowToForm);

        return $controls.append($editButton);
}
```

25. Save your changes and browse *index.html.*You should see *Edit* buttons in each row. Edit a row, and its value should fill the form, and the button change to *Update.*

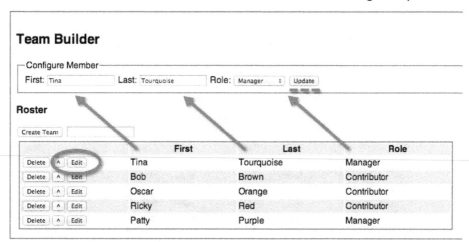

Replace existing rows with updated row

26. In *js/script.js,* review the code in the *$("#configureButton").click(...)* handler.

   - Prevent this form from submitting and capture the *button text* as *action*

```
event.preventDefault();
var action = $(this).text();
```

   - Select and get the form field values to create a *formData* object

```
var formData = {};
formData.firstName = $("input[name='firstName']").val();
formData.lastName = $("input[name='lastName']").val();
formData.role = $("select[name='role']").val();
formData.rowId = $("input[name='rowId']").val();
```

   - Create a new table *row* based on the form data

```
var $row = createRow(formData);
```

27. Below the existing code appending a new row, test *else if action* is *Update.*

28. In this condition, *.replaceAll()* elements matching the form *ID* with the new *$row.*

29. Clear the form, then *.find()* the button in the *configureMember* form and restore the button *.text()* from *Update* to *Create.*

30. Your code should look like this:

```
if(action === "Create") {
      $("#rosterTable").append($row)
      clearForm();
} else if(action === "Update") {

      $row.replaceAll("tr[id='" + formData.rowId + "']");
      clearForm();
      $("#configureMember").find("button").text("Create");
}
```

31. Save your changes and browse *index.html*. Select a row to *Edit*. Change its values. Press Update, and the changes should appear in the table.

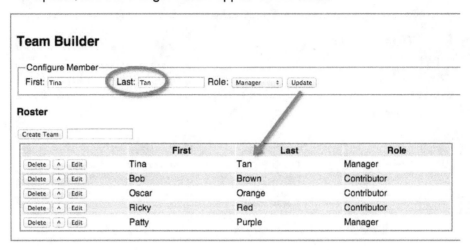

32. Close all project files.

Cloning and wrapping page elements

Cloning page elements and event handlers

Understanding the need

Content may need to be duplicated, to repeat elements on the page with or without changing the duplicated content. If the content includes non-visible elements, such as related data and event handlers, you need to ask whether those should be included in the duplicate.

For example, you may need to select specified rows, then wrap and display them as an indefinite number of new tables.

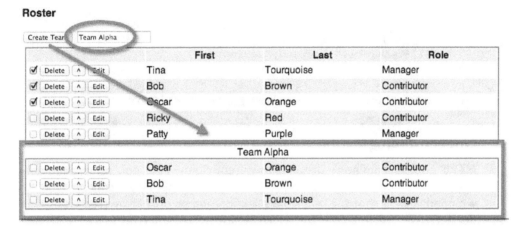

Cloning elements without related data and events

The *.clone()* method creates a deep copy of its selected content. Whether copying data and events is needed depends on the goal. By default, it does <u>not</u> copy data and events.

.clone() - create a deep copy of the selected element(s), <u>without</u> data and events

```
$(".duplicate").on("click", function(event) {
    $thisRow = $(event.target).parents("tr");
    $newRow = $thisRow.clone();
    $("#teamTable").append($newRow);
});
```

Cloning elements with related data and events

If .clone(true) is used, data and event handlers will still work for the duplicated content.

.clone(true) - create a deep copy of the selected element(s), <u>with</u> data and events

```
$(".duplicate").on("click", function(event) {
      $thisRow = $(event.target).parents("tr");
      $newRow = $thisRow.clone(true);
      $("#teamTable").append($newRow);
});
```

Wrapping elements with new markup

Understanding the need

HTML content commonly depends on parent elements to control layout and behavior. Table rows are wrapped by a table. Paragraphs may be wrapped by a container div. Image sets may be wrapped in an anchor tag to enable selection, and so on. Newly created or cloned elements may need to have additional markup applied before they can be displayed.

For example, you may wish to clone selected rows for display in a new table.

Roster

		First	Last	Role
☑ Delete ^ Edit		Tina	Tourquoise	Manager
☑ Delete ^ Edit		Bob	Brown	Contributor
☑ Delete ^ Edit		Oscar	Orange	Contributor
☐ Delete ^ Edit		Ricky	Red	Contributor
☐ Delete ^ Edit		Patty	Purple	Manager
	Team Alpha			
☐ Delete ^ Edit		Oscar	Orange	Contributor
☐ Delete ^ Edit		Bob	Brown	Contributor
☐ Delete ^ Edit		Tina	Tourquoise	Manager

Wrapping elements in new markup

jQuery supports four methods for wrapping (and unwrapping) elements. The markup to be wrapped may be specified as:

- a literal string of HTML markup

- a jQuery selector expression specifying other HTML markup

- a jQuery object defining other HTML markup

- a DOM element specifying other HTML markup

.wrap(markup) - wrap markup around each selected element

.wrapInner(markup) - wrap markup around the <u>content</u> of each selected element

.unwrap() - remove the parent element(s) around the selected element

.wrapAll(markup) - wrap common markup around the entire set of selected elements

Referencing newly wrapped elements

The wrapping methods modify their selected elements but do <u>not</u> return a jQuery object referring to the newly wrapped elements. If you wish to interact with the newly wrapped content, you must explicitly select it based on its new structure.

For example, if you wrap a set of table rows in a new table, you must select the newly created table element if you wish to append it for display.

```
<div id="container1">
  <table id="teamTable">
    <tr>
      <td><input type="checkbox"/></td>
      <td><button class="duplicate">Duplicate</button></td>
      <td><button class="edit">Edit</button></td><td>Oscar Orange</td></tr>
    <tr>
...
$("#createTable").on("click", function(event) {
      // select the rows surrounding checked boxes
      $selectedRows = $("input:checked").parents("tr");
      // clone the selected rows
      $clonedRows = $selectedRows.clone();
      // wrap the cloned rows in a table
      $wrappedRows = $clonedRows.wrapAll("<table/>");
      // get a reference to the newly created table
      $newTable = $wrappedRows.parents("table");
      // add the new table to the container
      $("#container1").append($newTable);
});
```

Exercise: Cloning and wrapping page elements

In this exercise you will take selected rows and wrap them to create and display a new table, with cloned event handlers.

After completion, you should be able to:

- Select a set of elements containing common child elements having the same state

- Clone elements with or without their event handlers

- Wrap selected elements in new elements

- Select newly wrapped elements, prepend additional children, and insert to the page

Steps

Review project files

1. Open the following project and review its starting files.

    `/ftjq/6-clone-wrap`

2. The files are identical to the completed state of the prior exercise.

Append checkboxes to enable multiple table row selection

3. In *js/script.js*, in the *createRow(item)* function, above the statement which appends a *Delete* button to the *$controls* cell, add a statement creating and appending a *checkbox* element with the *class team* to the *$controls* cell.

```
...
var $controls = $("<td class='controls'/>");
$controls.append($("<input type='checkbox' class='team' />"));
$controls = addDeleteButton($controls);
...
```

Note, elements append in order. Here, appending the checkbox first means it will appear on the left end of the controls cell. Also, note the .append() method expects a jQuery object as its argument.

4. Save your changes and browse *index.html*. You should see a *checkbox* in each row.

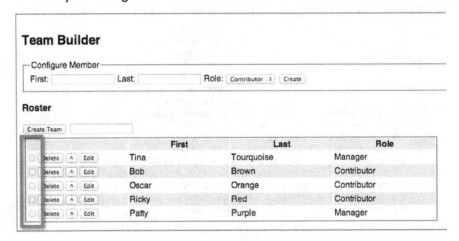

Clone rows to create new table

5. In *js/script.js*, in the *$("#createTeamButton").click()* event handler, notice that the *teamName* variable is populated when the *Create Team* button is clicked.

6. Below this statement, select all *:checked* elements of *class .team*, and assign their *.parents()* tr elements to a new local *var $selectedRows*.

7. Output *$selectedRows* to *console.log()*.

8. Your code should look like this:

```
$("#createTeamButton").click(function(event) {
    var teamName = $("input[name='teamName']").val();
    var $selectedRows = $(".team:checked").parents("tr");
    console.log($selectedRows);
});
```

9. Save your changes, browse *index.html*, open the browser console, check set of rows, then click the *Create Team* button. You should see the selected rows in the console.

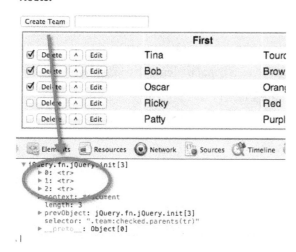

10. In *js/script.js*, below the previous statement, *.clone()* the *$selectedRows* and assign the result to a new local *var $clonedRows*.

11. Next, *.wrapAll()* of the *$selectedRows* in a new *table* element with *class tableDisplay*, select the *.parents()* table element which gets wrapped around the *$selectedRows*, and assign this table to a new local *var $newTable*.

12. Add a second *console.log()* statement displaying *$newTable*.

13. Your code should look like this:

```
$("#createTeamButton").click(function(event) {
  var teamName = $("input[name='teamName']").val();
  var $selectedRows = $(".team:checked").parents("tr");
  var $clonedRows = $selectedRows.clone();
  $newTable =
    $clonedRows.wrapAll("<table class='tableDisplay'/>").parents("table");

  console.log($selectedRows);
  console.log($newTable);
});
```

14. Save your changes, browse *index.html*, open the console, select a set of rows, and press *Create Table*. In the console, should see a table created from the selected rows.

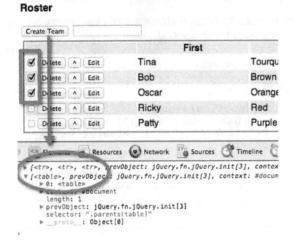

15. In *js/script.js*, comment out the *console.log()* statements just added above.

16. Next, *.prepend()* to *$newTable* a *caption* element to display the *teamName* value.

17. Insert *$newTable* after the *#rosterTable*.

18. Clear the form by unchecking the checkboxes, and setting "" as the *teamName .val()*.

19. Your code should look like this:

```
$("#createTeamButton").click(function(event) {
    ...
    $newTable.prepend("<caption>" + teamName + "</caption>");
    $newTable.insertAfter("#rosterTable");
    $(".team:checked").prop("checked", false);
    $("input[name='teamName']").val("");
    ...
});
```

20. Save your changes and browse *index.html*. Select a set of rows, assign a team name, and press *Create Team*. You should see a new table comprised of your selected rows displayed below the roster table.

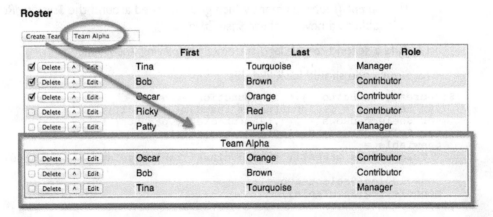

Clone event handlers in addition to markup

21. In the Team Builder application, attempt to delete, move, or edit a row in the new team table. It should not work, because only markup was cloned, not event handlers.

22. In *js/script.js*, in the *$("#createTeamButton").click()* event handler, modify the *.clone()* statement to pass the argument *true*.

```
$("#createTeamButton").click(function(event) {
    var teamName = $("input[name='teamName']").val();
    var $selectedRows = $(".team:checked").parents("tr");

    // clone event handlers as well as markup
    var $clonedRows = $selectedRows.clone(true);
    ..
```

23. Save your changes and browse *index.html*. Create a new team. The buttons in the new table should now work correctly.

24. Close all project files.

Introducing HTML templating

Understanding template solutions

Assembling page elements in JavaScript, even with jQuery, quickly becomes complex. Templates enable separation between data, and the presentation of that data.

In a template, a snippet of HTML is defined along with the locations where externally defined data properties should be displayed. As an example, a template might look like this:

```
<script id="rowTemplate" type="text/x-jquery-tmpl">
  <tr>
    <tr><td>${firstName}</td><td>${lastName}</td><td>${role}</td></tr>
  </tr>
</script>
```

Code using this template to populate a table named *teamTable* - possibly using JSON data exposing *firstName*, *lastName*, and *role* properties - might look like this:

```
$.getJSON("data/people.json", function(data) {
      $("#rowTemplate").tmpl(data).appendTo("#teamTable");
});
```

Using template solutions

jQuery does not, by itself, support templating. An official jQuery Template plugin was proposed, but never emerged from the beta process. It is now formally deprecated.

Many other templating solutions exist.

http://mustache.github.com/

http://www.jonnyreeves.co.uk/2012/using-external-templates-with-mustache-js-and-jquery/

The Underscore.js JavaScript function library also includes a templating function.

http://underscorejs.org/

A useful discussion on the state of jQuery templating, with references, can be found here:

http://stackoverflow.com/questions/170168/jquery-templating-engines

A history and roadmap of jQuery templating solutions can be found here:

http://www.borismoore.com/2011/10/jquery-templates-and-jsviews-roadmap.html

Summary

In this unit you have learned:

- There is no need to request a new page just to change layout

- New page elements are created by passing markup to the jQuery function

- Page elements can be
    - appended or prepended
    - inserted before or after
    - selected in relation as parent, child, or sibling
    - detached, removed, or emptied
    - cloned with or without data and events
    - wrapped with new markup

- Some page modification methods support both target-first and content-first variants

- New event handlers are assigned using *.on()* in favor of *.bind()* and *.live()* is deprecated

Review

1. You want an event handler to be assigned to specified elements whether they already exist or are created later. How do you do this?

2. You want to select all images of a certain class and assign a hyperlink to each one of them individually. How could you make this happen?

3. You have a set of images displayed in a row. You want to select one, then move it either closer to the start or end of the row. How could you do this?

4. You've created a container based layout to surround a form. You want to display a visually similar form below the first, but with different fields based on selections made in the first form. What are some approaches you might take to making this happen?

5. You want to change the layout surrounding a form without changing the form itself. How could you do this?

Objectives

After completing this unit, you should understand:

- How to add, remove, and trigger single and multiple use event handlers

- How to listen for multiple events with a single listener

- How to specify and use event namespaces

- Two ways to prevent default event behavior

- How events bubble up from parent to child

- How to filter and handle child events from a parent

- How to prevent events from bubbling

Using event-driven development

Introducing event handling

An event is a signal dispatched to indicate something happened, somewhere in the browser. Almost all events are ignored. Developers selectively choose which events are monitored ("listened") for and handled when they occur.

One way to understand event handling is to ask three questions.

- *What happened?* What was dispatched? A click event? Focus? Mouseover?

- *Who did it?* What object dispatched the event? A button object? Field? Div?

- *What now?* What code should run in response? An anonymous function? A named one?

Conceptually, listening and handling are two distinct tasks. A *listener* is the code monitoring a particular object for a particular event. A *handler* is the code which runs when it happens. In practice, little distinction is made and the two terms are often used interchangeably.

Surveying jQuery shorthand eventmethods

jQuery simplifies coding event handlers by providing shorthand methods for core events. In some cases (e.g., mouseenter) these events exist natively in some browsers, while being simulated by jQuery for other browsers, to achieve uniform behavior.

JavaScript Event	jQuery Shorthand
blur - element loses focus by mouse or tab	`.blur()`
change - user sets or selects a different value for the element	`.change()`
click - mousedown + mouseup over same element	`.click()`
dblclick - two clicks over the same element	`.dblclick()`
focus - elements receives focus by mouse or tab	`.focus()`
focusIn - element or a nested child receives focus by mouse or tab	`.focusIn()`
focusOut - element or a nested child loses focus by mouse or tab	`.focusOut()`
error - element dispatches error (e.g., img fails to load)	`.error()`
keydown - key pressed, dispatches before keypress	`.keydown()`
keypress - key pressed, dispatches after keydown	`.keypress()`
keyup - key released	`.keyup()`
load - element and all children including images have loaded	`.load()`
ready - DOM loaded but images may not yet be loaded	`.ready()`
unload - user is navigating away from the page	`.unload()`
mouseenter - mouse enters area of a specific element	`.mouseenter()`
mouseleave - mouse leaves area of a specific element	`.mouseleave()`
mouseover - pointer moves over an element or nested child	`.mouseover()`
mouseout - pointer moves off an element or nested child	`.mouseout()`
mouseup - button releases while mouse is over an element	`.mouseup()`
resize - browser window changes size	`.resize()`
scroll - position change in window, frame, or CSS overflowed element	`.scroll()`
select - text selected in text or textarea field	`.select()`
submit - user has submitted the target element's form	`.submit()`

Writing and using event handlers

Writing a basic event handler

The shorthand syntax to directly assign a jQuery event handler is:

selector.type(function(event){...});

Target - the object dispatching the event, or in some cases its enclosing parent

Type - the jQuery shorthand name (click, resize, keyup, etc.)

Handler - the function to be called and passed this event's event object

Understanding the event object

Event handling functions are passed an event object as an argument. This object supports numerous properties, which vary by context, but universally includes these:

type   the nature of the event (example: "click", "mouseover", etc.)

target   a reference to the object dispatching the event

currentTarget   a reference to the object from which the event is handled

The *target* and *currentTarget* properties will be different if events are allowed to "bubble up" to be handled from a parent element. Event bubbling is discussed later in this unit.

When using jQuery, the *event* object is often ignored, in favor of creating a jQuery object based on the *this* reference available in any event handler.

```
$("#submit").on("click", function(event){
    // these provide equivalent behavior
    // $(event.target).prop("disabled", "true");
    $(this).prop("disabled", "true");
});
```

Understanding the .on() method

Each of the jQuery shorthand methods relies on an underlying jQuery *.on()* method. As a result, this syntax may be used as an alternative for jQuery events:

*selector.**on**(type, function(event){...})***;**

The following two event handler assignments are equivalent.

```
// assign mouseover handler using shorthand
$("#container").mouseover(function(event) {
    // handle mouseover event
});
// assign mouseover handler using on
$("#container").on("mouseover", function(event) {
    // handle mouseover event
});
```

The *.on()* method allows an object's event type to be specified dynamically. For most browsers, though, there is little performance difference between these approaches, if any.

http://jsperf.com/shorthand-jquery-event-vs-on-event

Removing events with .off()

Event handlers may be removed at runtime using the *.off()* method.

*selector.**off**(type);*

All events of the specified type are removed from the target selector.

```
// each button works only once
<button class="strike">Strike 1</button>
<button class="strike">Strike 2</button>
<button class="strike">Strike 3</button>
<button id="disableAll">Disable All<button>
...
// remove click event handlers from .strike buttons
$("#disableAll").on("click", function() {
        $(".strike").off("click");
});
```

Handling events with anonymous vs. named functions

Handlers may be written anonymously inline with the corresponding listener.

```
$("#container").scroll(function(event) {
        // handle scroll event
});
```

Alternately, a separate function may be referenced. But, recall that JavaScript functions are objects. When assigning a separate event handler function, only an object reference is provided, not an explicit function call (no parentheses or arguments).

```
$("#container").scroll(scrollHandler);

function scrollHandler(event) {
        // handle scross event
}
```

Assigning named functions provides the benefit of using the same handler for multiple events, when this may be practical.

Binding multiple events

When using the *.on()* method to assign event handlers, multiple events may be passed as a space-delimited string.

For example, to trigger the same handler whether the window resizes or scrolls:

```
$(window).on("resize scroll", function(event) {
        // handle either resize or scroll
});
```

Using events one time only

Event handlers assigned using the *.one()* method are called no more than once for each element to which the event is assigned, and are then removed from that element.

*selector.**one(***type, function(eventObject) {...}**);**

Strike 1   Strike 2   Strike 3

Strike 1
Strike 2
Strike 3

```
// each button works only once
<button class="strike">Strike 1</button>
<button class="strike">Strike 2</button>
<button class="strike">Strike 3</button>
<p id="display" />
...
$(".strike").one("click", function(event) {
        $("#display").append($(this).text()).append("<br/>");
});
```

Setting the *disabled* property *true* also prevents event dispatching, and provides a visual effect.

Triggering events

The *.trigger()* method forces events of the selected target and type to be dispatched.

*selector.**trigger(***type**);**

Strike 1   Strike 2   Strike 3   Remove Handlers   Trigger 3 Strikes

Strike 1
Strike 2
Strike 3

```
<button class="strike">Strike 1</button>
<button class="strike">Strike 2</button>
<button class="strike">Strike 3</button>
<button id="removeHandlers">Remove Handlers</button>
<button id="triggerAll">Trigger 3 Strikes</button>
<p id="display" />
...
$(".strike").prop("disabled", "true");
$("#triggerAll").on("click", function(event) {
        // works even though buttons are disabled
        $(".strike").trigger("click");
});
```

Note, the *disabled* property prevents user input, but does not remove event handlers.

Using event namespaces with .on()

jQuery allows events to be assigned and referenced with "namespaces" - suffix identifiers separated from an event type by a dot (.) operator. Namespaces enable related events to be controlled, without impacting other events of the same type and selector.

*selector.on(type.**namespace**, function(){...});*
*selector.off(type.**namespace**);*
*selector.trigger(type.**namespace**);*

Play Ball!
Strike 1 Strike 2 Strike 3
Game Over.

```
<button id="start">Start Game</button>
<button class="strike">Strike 1</button>
<button class="strike">Strike 2</button>
<button class="strike">Strike 3</button>
<button id="end">End Game</button>
<p id="display" />
...
$(".strike").on("click.play", function(event) {
    $("#display").append($(this).text()).append("<br/>");
});
$("#start").on("click", function(event) {
    $("#display").append("Play Ball!<br/>");
});
$("#end").on("click", function(event) {
    $("#display").append("Game Over.<br/>");
    // turn off strike buttons, but not start button
    $("button").off("click.play");
});
```

Exercise: Adding, removing, and triggering events

In this exercise you will add, remove, and trigger single and multiple use event handlers on dynamically created objects, to enable a simple guessing game.

After completion, you should be able to:

- Understand single vs multiple use event handlers

- Remove unnecessary event handlers

- Trigger events on specified elements

Steps

Review project files

1. Open the following project and review its starting files.

   `/ftjq/7-event-handlers`

2. Briefly review index.html to notice:

   - Buttons named *newButton* and *checkButton*

   - Divs named *productsDiv* and *messageDiv*

3. Browse *index.html* through your local web server and notice its initial state.

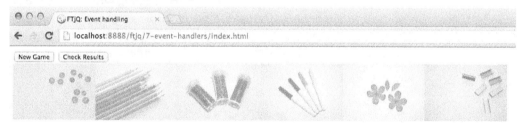

Note, this is a simple game in which the user guesses which two different images were randomly selected to win. Each image may be chosen only once per game, and the user chooses when to check her results. Pre-built code displays each game's winners in the JavaScript console.

4. The implementation details are not important to this exercise, but briefly review *js/script.js* to notice:

   - pre-built *loadProductImages()* loads data, configure img elements with *data*, *class*, and *width*, displays them in *productsDiv*, then fades *productsDiv* using CSS *opacity*.

   - pre-built *setNewGame()*, *chooseWinners()*, and *handleImageClick()* functions manage play and display, along with a pre-built *$("#checkButton").click* handler

Implement an event handler to assign other event handlers

5. In *js/script.js*, add a *click* event handler for *newButton*.

6. In this handler, call the pre-built *setNewGame()* function.

7. Assign each *img* element of the *product* class a *one*-time only event listener which calls the pre-built *handleImageClick()* function as its event handler.

8. Your code should look like this:

```
$("#newButton").on("click", function(event){
    setNewGame();
        $("img.product").one("click", handleImageClick);
});
```

9. Save your changes and browse *index.html*. Open the JavaScript console. Click the *New Game* button. Click on images (you can force a win by choosing the products shown in the console). Notice you can only choose each product once. Then, click the *Check Results* button.

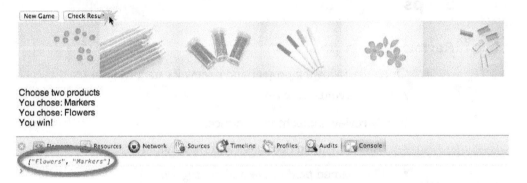

10. Next, click on *New Game* to start a second game. Notice that clicking any product not clicked in the previous game displays its choice twice, though you only see this effect happen one time for each such image. Play a third game, and previously unclicked products should display their choice three times, and so on.

Remove unneeded event handlers

11. In *js/script.js*, in the *$("#newButton").click* event handler, remove all click handlers from the product images before assigning new ones.

```
$("#newButton").on("click", function(event){
    setNewGame();
        $("img.product").off("click");
        $("img.product").one("click", handleImageClick);
});
```

12. Save your changes and browse *index.html*. Play a new game, then check the results. Play a second new game. Each image should respond to only one click event.

Configure multiple events per handler

13. In *js/script.js*, modify the product image event handler to respond to both *click* and *mouseover* events.

14. Also, modify the code so that each event handler can be used multiple times.

```
$("#newButton").on("click", function(event){
    setNewGame();
    $("img.product").off("click");
    $("img.product").on("click mouseover", handleImageClick);
});
```

15. Save your changes and browse *index.html*. You now both roll over and click images to select them.

Trigger an event to start an initial game

16. In *js/script.js*, in the *$.getJSON* anonymous callback function inside the *loadProductImages()* function, trigger a *click* event on *newButton* immediately after product images have been loaded into *productsDiv*.

```
function loadProductImages() {
    $.getJSON("data/products.json", function(data) {
        ...
        $.each(data, function(index, item){
            ...
        });

        $("#newButton").trigger("click");
    });
    ...
```

17. Save your changes and browse *index.html*. A new game should be ready to play as soon as you load the page.

Choose two products

18. Close all project files.

Using the event object

Understanding the event object

The JavaScript event object is the first argument passed to event handlers. It identifies what happened and who did it. jQuery normalizes the following event object properties to ensure cross-browser consistency.

target - reference to element that dispatched this event

relatedTarget - additional DOM element(s) involved in event

pageX - mouse position relative to left edge of document

pageY - mouse position relative to top edge of document

which - for key/mouse events, the specific key pressed

metakey - boolean true|false whether meta key was pressed when event dispatched

The following are also copied onto the event object, but may or may not be populated based on browser and event type: *altKey, bubbles, button, cancelable, charCode, clientX, clientY, ctrlKey, currentTarget, data, detail, eventPhase, offsetX, offsetY, originalTarget, prevValue, screenX, screenY, shiftKey, target, view*.

Referencing the dispatching object

Commonly, event handlers will modify or interact the object dispatching the event. Recall that a jQuery object can be selected using the JavaScript this reference. This object can access any element property using *.prop(name[, value])* method, *.text()* method, *.val()* method, and so on.

```
<table>
        <tr><td>1</td><td>2</td><td>3</td></tr>
        <tr><td>4</td><td>6</td><td>7</td></tr>
        <tr><td>7</td><td>8</td><td>9</td></tr>
</table>
...
$("td").on("click", function(event){
        clickedNumber = $(this).text();
});
```

Preventing default behavior

Calling *.preventDefault()* on an event object suppresses the built-in behavior which would otherwise be triggered. For example, prevent form submission in a submit button click handler. Or, prevent page loading in an anchor tag click handler.

```
$("#submitForm").on("click", function(event) {
        event.preventDefault();
});
```

Understanding event bubbling

Because events "bubble up", they may be handled from a dispatching element's enclosing parent. This is useful in minimizing the number of event handlers created and managed by the browser. No special syntax is required, it's a matter of placement.

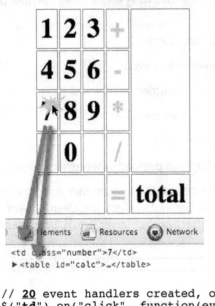

```
// 20 event handlers created, one for each td
$("td").on("click", function(event){
        console.log(this);
});
// 1 event handler created for the table
$("table").on("click", function(event){
        console.log(this);
});
```

Filtering events for desired targets

An optional argument can be set when assigning event handlers for a nesting (parent) element. This argument causes jQuery to listen only for events from a specified type or types of nested (child) elements.

*selector.on(event, **filter**, function(event){...});*

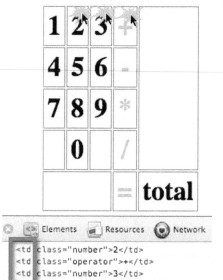

```
// 1 event handler created for this table
$("table").on("click", "td", function(event){
      console.log(this);
});
```

Suppressing event bubbling

Calling the *.stopPropagation()* method on an event object prevents the event from bubbling up through parent elements.

```
$("td.number").on("click", function(event) {
      event.stopPropagation();
});
```

Both default behavior and event bubbling can be suppressed by ending a function with return false. Opinions vary on whether explicit method calls or return false are the better approach.

```
$("#submit").on("click", function(event) {
      // suppress both form submission and event bubbling
      event.preventDefault();
      event.stopPropagation();
      // or
      return false
});
```

Examining event handlers created by jQuery

Event handlers can be examined in the *Elements* tab, or similar location, of the web browser developer tools. Set the tool to display *Selected Node Only* to examine actual event handlers created, rather than *All Nodes* for which a given event handler will run.

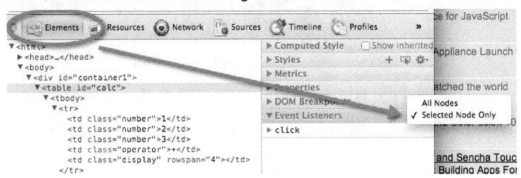

Exercise: Controlling default behavior and minimizing handlers

In this exercise you implement event handlers with three different selector approaches to see how many handlers are created, the effective event area, and to control default event behavior.

After completion, you should be able to:

- Suppress default event behavior

- Rely on filtered events handled on parent elements to minimize handler creation

Steps

Review project files

1. Open the following project and review its starting files.

   `/ftjq/7-event-bubbling`

2. Briefly review *index.html* to notice

   - *td* elements of *class number* and *operator*

   - *td* elements with *id display* and *result*

3. Browse *index.html* and click a number to see its initial state. The calculator should function, but a popup should appear, interfering with using it.

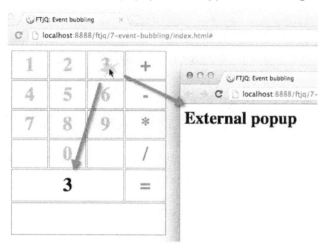

External popup

4. The calculator details are not critical, but briefly review *js/script.js* to notice:

   - the text within *number* and *operator class td* elements is wrapped in anchor tags, which in turn have the *numberAnchor* and *operatorAnchor class*

```
$(".number").wrapInner("<a href='popup.html' target='new'
    class='numberAnchor' />");
$(".operator").wrapInner("<a href='popup.html' target='new'
    class='operatorAnchor' />");
```

   - pre-built *click* handlers for elements of the *numberAnchor* and *operatorAnchor class* are defined, implementing simple calculator behavior

Suppress default behavior

5. In both the *$(".numberAnchor").click* and *$(".operatorAnchor").click* handlers, use the *event* object to prevent the anchor tags from loading the popup.

```
$(".numberAnchor").on("click", function(event){
    event.preventDefault();
    ...

$(".operatorAnchor").on("click", function(event){
    event.preventDefault();
    ...
```

6. Save your changes and browse *index.html*. The popup should no longer interfere with the calculator. However, also notice you must precisely select text to trigger an event.

Note, if the goal is to use anchor tags for event triggering *only*, set *<a href="#">text</a>*.

Increase response area using td events

7. In *js/script.js*, modify the *$(".numberAnchor").click* handler to listen for *click* events on *td* elements of the *number* class, instead of anchor events. (Simply comment out the existing function signature, and write a new signature above it.)

```
$("td.number").on("click", function(event) {
// $(".numberAnchor").on("click", function(event){
    event.preventDefault();
    ...
```

8. Comment out the statement assigning anchor tags to *number class* elements.

```
// $(".number").wrapInner("<a href='popup.html' target='new'
    class='numberAnchor' />");
```

9. Save your changes and browse *index.html*. Because of how jQuery implements the *.text()* method of the jQuery object, the calculator should still work as written. However, now the entire table cell for *number class* elements can be clicked for its value (though for *operator class* elements, the text must still be clicked, as these were not changed.)

10. Open your browser's developer tools. Configure the tool to display events for selected nodes only. Examine the calculator table, and notice that a unique event handler has been created and assigned to each *td* element.

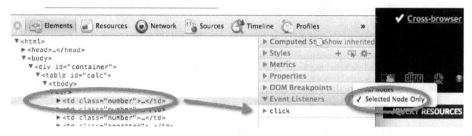

Use event bubbling to minimize event handler count

11. In *js/script.js*, modify the *$("td.number").click* handler to listen for *click* events on the *table* itself, but filtered for only those dispatched by *number class td* elements. (Simply comment out the existing function signature, and write a new signature above it.)

```
$("table").on("click", "td.number", function(event) {
// $("td.number").on("click", function(event) {
// $(".numberAnchor").on("click", function(event){
    event.preventDefault();
    ...
```

12. Save your changes and browse index.html. Again, because of how jQuery implements the *.text()* method of the jQuery object, the calculator should still work as written, because the only elements triggering events are *td.number* elements.

13. Open your browser's developer tools. Verify the tool is displaying events for selected nodes only. Examine the calculator table, and notice that only the *table* element has a *click* event (along with *td.operator* elements, which have not been changed).

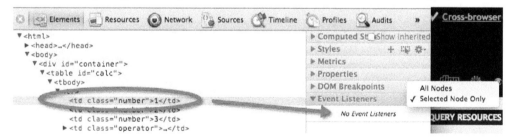

14. Close all project files.

Summary

In this unit you have learned:

- jQuery provides standard cross-browser behavior for its events

- Shorthand event listeners rely on the *selector.on(type, function)* method

- Event listeners can be removed using *selector.off(type)* method

- Event handlers may be written anonymously inline with the listener assignment, or as named functions

- Single-use events can be created using the *selector.one(type, function)* method

- Specific events can be fired using the *selector.trigger(type)* method

- Event handlers are passed an object to identify the *type*, *target*, and other event-specific properties

- The *event.preventDefault()* method suppresses normal behavior (form submission, page load, etc.)

- Events bubble up from child to parent and may be handled by the parent

- The *event.stopPropagation()* method prevents event bubbling from child to parent

- The jQuery *selector.on(type[, filter], function)* method allows parent elements to choose which child events it will handle

Review

1. You want three specific elements to each handle their events the exact same way. How could you do this?

2. You want the user to select one, and only one, item in a list. How could you do this?

3. You want mousing over an image to have the same effect as clicking a specific button. What are some ways to do this?

4. You notice an event handler appears to be firing more than once for a particular event on a particular element. What may be happening, and how would you stop this?

5. Your users need to click on one of 100 different *div* elements on the page. What are some ways to avoid burdening the browser with 100 event handlers in memory?

Unit 8
Working with the jQuery UI library

Objectives

After completing this unit, you should understand:

- The general approach taken in creating jQuery plugins

- Configuring and integrating a version of the jQuery UI library, and its theme

- Implementing and configuring jQuery UI Interactions in general

- Integrating jQuery UI selectable and sortable interactions in the same element

- Implementing and configuring jQuery UI Widgets in general

- Implementing the markup and code for Menu, Accordion, and Tabs widgets

Introducing jQuery UI and jQuery

jQuery UI is a curated set of user interface *interactions*, *widgets*, *effects*, and *themes*, all built on the the core jQuery library.

Main site:
http://www.jQueryUI.com

Documentation:

http://API.jQueryUI.com

Introducing jQuery plugins

A jQuery "plugin" is an extension to the jQuery prototype (jQuery aliases "prototype" to "fn").

In its most simple form, a plugin could look like this:

```
jQuery.fn.myNewPlugin = function(foo) {
        console.log(foo);
};
```

Elsewhere, this function could be invoked like other jQuery functions:

```
$.myNewPlugin("Fred"); // writes "Fred" to the console
```

Commonly, a plugin would actually be a set of interrelated extensions, distributed and included within a page as a library - a JavaScript file - just like jQuery itself. Numerous extensions are available, including those created by the jQuery project, such as jQuery UI.

http://plugins.jQuery.com/

Solving problems using jQuery UI

jQuery UI is a plugin library focused on *interactions*, *widgets*, *effects*, all built on a common *core*, implementing a common *theme*, and based on jQuery and related *utilities*. Specific elements and a theme are chosen when building a version of the jQuery plugin library for download.

>   *Interactions* - visual behaviors

>   *Widgets* - visual tools with related behaviors

>   *Effects* - configurable "plug and play" animations

jQuery UI enables (relatively) easy creation of a richer user experience through a widely used and actively maintained open source library.

http://www.jQueryUI.com

Surveying the jQuery UI library

Interactions	Draggable	Droppable	Resizable
	Selectable	Sortable	
Widgets	Accordion	Autocomplete	Button
	Datepicker	Dialog	Menu
	Progressbar	Slider	Spinner
	Tabs	Tooltip	
Effects	Add Class	Color Animation	Effect
	Hide	Remove Class	Show
	Switch Class	Toggle	Toggle Class

Demonstrations of each are available online at:

http://jQueryUI.com/Demos/

Creating and deploying a version of the jQuery UI library

As fast as network speeds and JavaScript processing have become, it is still bad practice to load more code than needed into the browser. jQuery UI enables granular library build and theming, with dependency management, to create a download specific to the needs of your application.

To build a jQuery library:

1. Browse to http://jqueryui.com/download/

2. Uncheck *Toggle All*

3. Check the specifically desired *Interaction(s)*, *Widget(s)*, and *Effect(s)*

    • notice that dependencies are managed for you

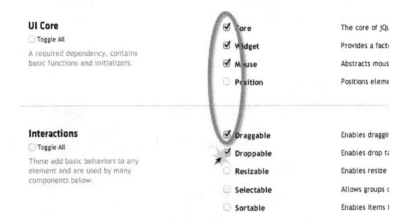

4. Select a *Theme* and provide an optional *CSS Scope*

    • CSS Scopes enable implementing multiple themes on a single page

5. Click *Download*

6. Extract the resulting archive to your project's JavaScript folder

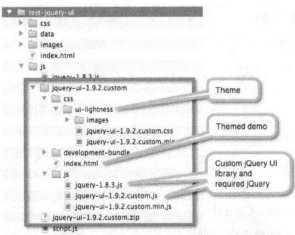

7. Link the files to the target page

Linking jQuery UI library files to the page

jQuery UI deployment relies on three main files. Like jQuery itself, jQuery UI may be deployed using either a fully displayed or minified version of the code.

1. CSS theme file

```
<link href="js/jquery-ui-1.10.0.custom/
  css/ui-lightness/jquery-ui-1.10.0.custom.css" rel="stylesheet">
```

2. jQuery file

```
<script
  src="js/jquery-ui-1.10.0.custom/js/jquery-1.9.0.js"></script>
```

3. jQuery UI file

```
<script
  src="js/jquery-ui-1.10.0.custom/js/jquery-ui-1.10.0.custom.js"></script>
```

Actual deployment folders will vary. It may be helpful but is not necessary to maintain the top-level version folder. In general, scripts should be linked in this sequence:

1. jQuery library

2. jQuery UI library

3. Project-specific scripts and libraries

Deploying jQuery UI from a Content Distribution Network

Due to browser caching, loading jQuery UI from a CDN may provide better page performance. This benefit can be weighed against directly deploying a potentially smaller custom library.

jQuery UI provides CDN deployment, with current release paths displayed at bottom of the Download Builder page.

Google also provides CDN access to jQuery and jQuery UI.

https://developers.google.com/speed/libraries/devguide

Considering when to use jQuery UI

Even with the ability to create selectively configured libraries, and optimize the user load experience by using a commonly cached CDN version of the library, jQuery may provide more functionality - and file weight - than desired. Factors to weight include:

- file weight relative to target audience network speed

- usability of CDN-cached jQuery UI for the project

- complexity of maintaining custom code or less widely adopted libraries

jQuery UI 1.9 was recently released in preparation for the planned jQuery 2.0 release.

- jQuery 2.0 will drop support for non-standards compliant browsers (such as IE6) resulting in much lower library file size

- jQuery 1.9 will maintain current backwards compatibility, with corresponding file weight

Introducing jQuery themes

jQuery UI separates the display and behavior of its visual elements through the use of CSS styling and related image assets. Pre-built themes are available to select during download.

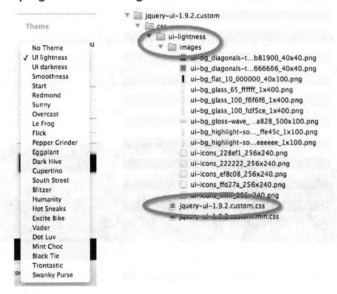

Custom themes can also be developed and deployed using the jQuery UI ThemeRoller tool.

http://jQueryUI.com/Themeroller/

Enhancing interactivity

Introducing jQuery UI interactions

Interactions add mouse-based interaction to any element. They can used alone, or in combination to create more complex behaviors, custom widgets, and applications.

Interactions	Draggable	Droppable	Resizable
	Selectable	Sortable	

High level demonstrations of each interaction can be found here:

http://jQueryUI.com/Demos/

Documentation of interactions and techniques can be found here:

http://api.jQueryui.com/

Understanding the general implementation approach

jQuery UI interactions are applied to HTML elements which have been assigned the CSS class *ui-widget-content*.

```
<div id="dragTarget" class="ui-widget-content">
      <p>Some content</p>
</div>
...
$("#dragTarget").draggable();
```

Applying interactions to sets of elements and configuring options

An interaction will apply to all children of the element to which it is applied. Child elements can be assigned the *ui-widget-content class*, and a *filter* option applied, to specify which particular child elements which should have the desired interaction.

All jQuery UI elements are configurable by *options*, such as the *filter* option, commonly passed as an inline object argument to the method enabling the interaction.

```
<table id="peopleTable">
      <tr><th>First</th><th>Last</th><th>Role</th>
      </tr>
      <tr class="ui-widget-content">
            <td class="firstName">Tina</td>
            <td class="lastName">Tourquoise</td>
            <td class="role">Manager</td>
      </tr>
      <tr class="ui-widget-content">
            <td class="firstName">Bob</td>
                  ...
$("#peopleTable").selectable({filter:"tr"});
```

Handling interaction events

Many jQuery UI event names are preceded by the widget or interaction name. For example, the *selected* event of the *selectable* interaction is implemented as *.on("selectableselected", ...)*.

However, this naming approach is not consistent in the most current releases. For example, the *sort* event of the *sortable* interaction is implemented as *.on("sort", ...)*.

Interaction events dispatch for <u>each</u> element involved in the interaction. For example, if 3 items are selected, a *selected* event will be dispatched 3 times, once for each item selected.

```
$("#sourceList").on("selectableselected", function(event, ui){
      // copy the selected list item
      $item = $(ui.selected).clone();
      // add the list item to the second list
      $("#targetList").append($item);
});
```

Source List

- Apple
- Banana
- Cherry
- Date
- Elderberry

Target List

- Banana
- Cherry
- Date

Understanding the ui argument

Interaction event handlers are passed both *event* and *ui* arguments. The *ui* argument is populated with one or more properties representing the target(s) of the event. The specific properties of *ui*, and the objects they expose, will vary by event.

```
$("#sourceList").on("sort", function(event, ui){
      console.log(ui);
};
```

For example, in a *selected* event for a *selectable* interaction, *ui* has a *selected* property referring to the selected item.

In a *sort* event for a *sortable* interaction, *ui* has several properties: *helper*, *item*, *offset*, *position*, *originalPosition*, and *sender*.

See the documentation for the specific structure of the UI object for each interaction event.

http://api.jQueryUI.com/Category/Interactions/

Making elements selectable

The *selectable* interaction provides a uniform way to determine which elements users choose.

Options	appendTo	autoRefresh	cancel
	delay	disabled	distance
	filter	tolerance	
Methods	destroy	disable	enable
	refresh	option	widget
Events	create	selected	selecting
	start	stop	unselected
	unselecting		

http://api.jQueryUI.com/Selectable/

Implementing and styling the selectable interaction

Commonly, the selectable interaction will be applied to a group of elements, enabling the user to specify their choice or choices. Many styles can be specified. Most importantly ui-selecting and ui-selected styles are assigned to control how elements appear during and after selection.

```
#selectList .ui-selecting {
      background: #00ee00;
}
#selectList .ui-selected {
      background: #00cc00;
}
...
<ul id="selectList">
      <li class="ui-widget-content">Apple</li>
      <li class="ui-widget-content">Banana</li>
      <li class="ui-widget-content">Cherry</li>
      <li class="ui-widget-content">Date</li>
      <li class="ui-widget-content">Elderberry</li>
</ul>
...
$("#selectList").selectable();
```

- Apple
- Banana
- Cherry
- Date
- Elderberry

Configuring a selectable interaction

The interaction can be configured with a set of *options* controlling its behavior.

Options	appendTo	autoRefresh	cancel
	delay	disabled	distance
	filter	tolerance	

Similar to other jQuery tools, options are commonly set by passing an inline object to the interaction method.

```
<ul id="selectList">
      <li class="ui-widget-content">Apple</li>
      <li class="ui-widget-content, cancel">Banana</li>
      <li class="ui-widget-content">Cherry</li>
</ul>
...
$("#selectList").selectable({
                      cancel:"a, .cancel",
                      delay: 250,
                      });
```

Handling selectable events

The *selectable* interaction exposes events to manage the selection life cycle.

Events	create	selected	selecting
	start	stop	unselected
	unselecting		

The *selectable* interaction events include the interaction name when implementing the event.

```
$("#sourceList").on("selectableselected", function(event, ui){
      // handle selection
});
```

Exercise: Implementing jQuery UI and creating a selectable interaction

In this exercise you will create a table supporting simultaneous editing of selected rows.

After completion, you should be able to:

- Configure and download a custom jQuery UI library

- Implement the Selectable interaction

- Filter selection to desired child elements

- Understand the UI object passed to interaction events

- Access values within selected elements

- Handle pre and post selection events

Steps

Review project files

1. Open the following project and review its starting files.

   `/ftjq/8-implement-interaction`

2. In *index.html*, notice these elements:

   - two tables *peopleTable* and *editTable*

   - *td* table cells of the *firstName*, *lastName*, and *role class*

   - jQuery *<script>* import is missing

3. In the */js* folder, notice *jquery-ui-1.10.0.custom-PROVIDED.zip*, which may be used if live access to *jQueryUI.com* is not available for this exercise.

Build and download a custom jQuery UI library

4. Browse to this URL:

   `http://www.jqueryui.com/download`

5. Configure a jQuery UI library for Interactions, only.

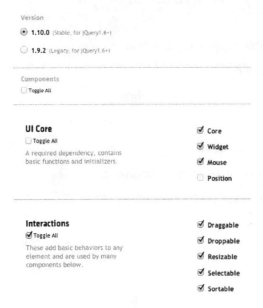

6. (Optional) Choose an alternate theme to *ui-lightness*.

7. Download the library archive to the */js* folder of the project.

8. Extract the archive in the */js* folder, keeping the library version folder.

Configure page to use jQuery UI library

9. In *index.html*, in the *head* element, add a *link* element for the custom library CSS file, above the current *link* to the project CSS file.

```
<head>
  <title>FTjQ: Implementing jQuery UI Interaction</title>
  <link rel="stylesheet" type="text/css"
    href="js/jquery-ui-1.10.0.custom/css
      /ui-lightness/jquery-ui-1.10.0.custom.css">
  <link rel="stylesheet" type="text/css" href="css/style.css" />
</head>
```

Note, your library version may vary from the version show in this exercise.

10. Above the *script* element for *js/script.js*, add a *script* element for the jQuery release included with this library.

11. Below the jQuery *script* element, and above the *script* element for *js/script.js*, add a *script* element for the jQuery UI library.

12. Your code should look like this:

```
<script type="text/javascript"
  src="js/jquery-ui-1.10.0.custom/js/jquery-1.9.0.js"></script>
<script type="text/javascript"
  src="js/jquery-ui-1.10.0.custom/js/jquery-ui-1.10.0.custom.js"></script>
<script type="text/javascript"
  src="js/script.js"></script>
</body>
</html>
```

Configure CSS for jQuery UI Interaction

13. In *index.html*, in the *peopleTable* element, add the *ui-widget-content class* to each table row other than the header row.

```
<table id="peopleTable" class="tableDisply">
    <tr>
            <th>First</th>
            <th>Last</th>
            <th>Role</th>
    </tr>
    <tr class="ui-widget-content">
            <td class="firstName">Tina</td>
            ...
```

14. In *css/style.css*, configure *ui-selecting* and *ui-selected* classes with these properties.

```
#peopleTable .ui-selecting {
    background: #33cc33;
}
#peopleTable .ui-selected {
    background: #00cc33;
}
```

Configure selectable interaction for table rows only

15. In *js/script.js*, call the *.selectable(options)* on a jQuery object for *peopleTable*

16. Filter the interaction to select table rows only, by passing *tr* as a *filter* property in an inline options object passed as an argument to the *.selectable(options)* method.

17. Your code should look like this:

```
$(document).ready(function() {

    $("#peopleTable").selectable({filter:"tr"});

    ...
```

18. Save your changes and browse the page. You should be able to both single and multiple select table rows. Selecting and selected rows should change *background-color* and *color* as specified by the *ui-selecting* and *ui-selected* classes.

First	Last	Role
Tina	Tourquoise	Manager
Bob	Brown	Contributor
Krishna	Kohl	Contributor
Oscar	Orange	Contributor
Ricky	Red	Manager
Patty	Purple	Manager

Handle selected events to enable multi-row editing

19. In *js/script.js*, handle the *selectableselected* event for the *peopleTable*, capturing both an *event* and ui object as arguments.

20. Create a jQuery object from the *ui.selected* property, and assign it to *$selectedRow*.

21. Your code should look like this:

```
$("#peopleTable").selectable({filter:"tr"});

    $("#peopleTable").on("selectableselected", function(event, ui){
        $selectedRow = $(ui.selected);
        console.log(ui);
        console.log($selectedRow);
    });
    ...
```

22. Save your changes and browse the code. Open the JavaScript console. Examine the log output for the ui argument, and the jQuery object created from its *ui.selected* property. Specifically notice the *children* elements and their classes.

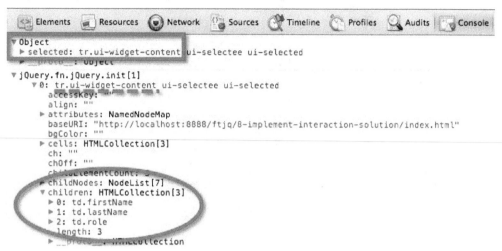

23. Using the *$selectedRow* object, *.find()* each of the *td.firstName*, *td.lastName*, and *td.role* elements, and assign their *.text()* to correspondingly named variables.

24. Copy, paste, and uncomment the pre-built code - which assigns the *firstName*, *lastName*, and *role* values to editable fields in a new table row appended to the *editTable* in *index.html* - into the *selectableselected* event handler.

25. Your code should look like this:

```
$("#peopleTable").on("selectableselected", function(event, ui){
    $selectedRow = $(ui.selected);
    console.log(ui);
    console.log($selectedRow);

    firstName = $selectedRow.find("td.firstName").text();
    lastName = $selectedRow.find("td.lastName").text();
    role = $selectedRow.find("td.role").text();

    $editRow = $("<tr>")
    $("<input type='text'name='firstName'/>").val(firstName)
        .appendTo("<td/>").appendTo($editRow);
    $("<input type='text'name='lastName'/>").val(lastName)
        .appendTo("<td/>").appendTo($editRow);
    $("<input type='text'name='role'/>").val(role)
        .appendTo("<td/>").appendTo($editRow);
        $editRow.appendTo("#editTable");

});
```

26. Save your changes and browse *index.html*. Select one or more rows, and corresponding editable rows should appear with the selected values. However, notice that because rows are not being cleared out, copies of the same row are appearing.

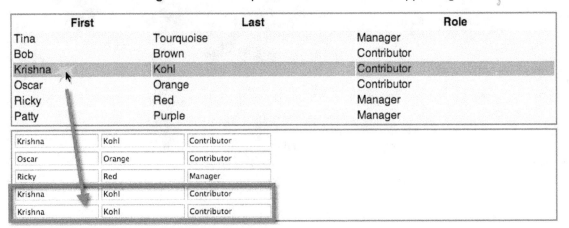

Handle selecting events on the selectable table

27. Add a *selectableselecting* event on the *peopleTable*.

28. In this event, *.empty()* all elements from the *editTable*.

29. Your code should look like this:

```
$("#peopleTable").on("selectableselecting", function(event, ui) {
    $("#editTable").empty();
});
```

30. Save your changes and browse *index.html*. Only current rows should be editable.

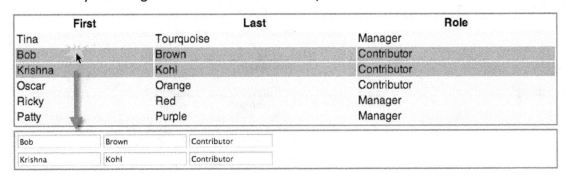

31. Close all project files.

Making elements sortable

The *sortable* interaction provides a uniform way to move items in a set among one another.

Options	appendTo	axis	cancel	connectWith	containment
	cursor	cursorAt	delay	disabled	distance
	dropOnEmpty	force HelperSize	force PlaceholderSize	grid	handle
	helper	items	opacity	placeholder	revert
	scroll	scrollSensitivity	scrollSpeed	tolerance	zIndex
Methods	cancel	destroy	disable	enable	refresh
	refresh Positions	serialize	toArray	widget	
Events	create	start	sort	change	beforeStop
	stop	update	receive	remove	over
	out	activate	deactivate		

http://api.jQueryUI.com/Sortable/

Implementing and styling the sortable interaction

Like the *selectable* interaction, the *sortable* interaction is applied to the common parent of a set of elements to be sorted.

```
<ul id="sourceList">
    <li class="ui-widget-content">Apple</li>
    <li class="ui-widget-content">Banana</li>
    <li class="ui-widget-content">Cherry</li>
    <li class="ui-widget-content">Date</li>
    <li class="ui-widget-content">Elderberry</li>
</ul>
...
$("#sourceList").sortable();
```

* Banana
  * Apple
* Cherry
* Date
* Elderberry

Configuring a sortable interaction

While the sortable interaction supports many options, one in specific helps integrate this interaction with others.

Options					
	appendTo	axis	cancel	connectWith	containment
	cursor	cursorAt	delay	disabled	distance
	dropOnEmpty	force HelperSize	force PlaceholderSize	grid	handle
	helper	items	opacity	placeholder	revert
	scroll	scrollSensitivity	scrollSpeed	tolerance	zIndex

The *handle* option enables a specific element within the sortable element to serve as the "handle" from which it may be chosen for sorting.

```
<ul id="sourceList">
  <li class="ui-widget-content"><span class="handle">X</span> Apple</li>
  <li class="ui-widget-content"><span class="handle">X</span> Banana</li>
  <li class="ui-widget-content"><span class="handle">X</span> Cherry</li>
  <li class="ui-widget-content"><span class="handle">X</span> Date</li>
  <li class="ui-widget-content"><span class="handle">X</span> Elderberry</li>
</ul>
...
$("#sourceList").sortable({handle:".handle"});
```

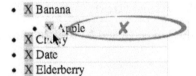

Handling sortable events

The *sortable* interaction exposes events to manage the sorting life cycle.

Events					
	create	start	sort	change	beforeStop
	stop	update	receive	remove	over
	out	activate	deactivate		

The *sortable* events do <u>not</u> include the interaction name when implementing the event.

```
$("#sourceList").on("sort", function(event, ui){
      // handle selection
});
```

Exercise: Integrating selectable and sortable interactions

In this exercise you will implement the sortable interaction to a table also using the selectable interaction, adding a handle, event, and fixed helper row to integrate the two interactions.

After completion, you should be able to:

- Implement the sortable interaction

- Assign a handle element to control the sort behavior

- Trigger an interaction event from a related interaction event

- Implement a modified visual helper for use during sorting

Steps

Review project files

1. Open the following project and review its starting files.

    `/ftjq/8-integrate-sortable`

2. While behavior is identical to the prior exercise, notice in *index.html* and *js/script.js*:

    - *peopleTable* contains only a header row

    - *peopleTable* is populated by *data/people.json*

    - a fourth table cell of *class handle* is added

```
$.getJSON("data/people.json", function(data){
  $.each(data, function(index, item){
    $row = $("<tr/>").addClass("ui-widget-content");
    $("<td/>").addClass("handle").text("> ").appendTo($row);
    $("<td/>").addClass("firstName").text(item.firstName).appendTo($row);
    $("<td/>").addClass("lastName").text(item.lastName).appendTo($row);
    $("<td/>").addClass("role").text(item.role).appendTo($row);
    $row.appendTo("#peopleTable");
  });
});
```

Implement the sortable interaction

3. In *js/script.js*, select the *tbody* element of *peopleTable* to create a jQuery object.

4. Call the *.sortable()* method on this object.

5. Your code should look like this:

```
$("#peopleTable tbody").sortable();
```

6. Save your changes and browse *index.html.* You should be able to select and drag the rows for sorting. However, the selectable interaction is no longer working.

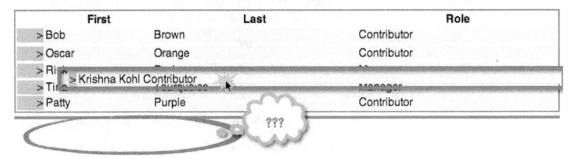

Assign a sort handle to solve interaction conflict

7. In *js/script.js,* pass an inline options object to the *.sortable()* method, assigning the *td* element with *class handle* as the *handle* value for the *.sortable()* method.

```
$("#peopleTable tbody").sortable({handle:"td.handle"});
```

8. Save your changes and browse *index.html.* The selectable behavior should work again, and sorting should only occur when clicking on the first cell of each row.

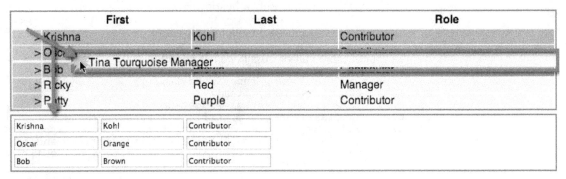

Trigger a related event at the end of each sort

9. In *js/script.js,* add a *sortstop* event handler to *$("#peopleTable tbody").*

10. In the handler, *.trigger()* the *selectableselecting* event on *peopleTable,* so that *editTable* is emptied if *peopleTable* has been sorted.

11. Your code should look like this:

```
$("#peopleTable tbody").sortable({handle:"td.handle"});

$("#peopleTable tbody").on("sortstop", function(event){
    $("#peopleTable").trigger("selectableselecting");
});
```

12. Save your changes and browse *index.html.* The *editTable* should clear after each sort.

Improve the appearance of the drag helper

13. In *js/script.js*, create a *fixHelper* function with *event* and *ui* arguments.

14. Assign the *.children()* of the *ui* argument to *$originalRow*.

15. Assign a *.clone()* of the *ui* argument to *$helperRow*.

16. Loop over *.each()* of the *.children()* of *$helperRow*, passing the *index* and *item* for each loop iteration to its function.

17. Assign the *.width()* of the *$originalRow* at this *index* as the *.width()* of *$(this)* particular helper row child currently in the loop.

18. After the loop, *return* the improved *$helperRow*.

19. Your code should look like this:

```
function fixHelper(event, ui) {
        var $originalRow = ui.children();
        var $helperRow = ui.clone();
        $helperRow.children().each(function(index, item){
                $(this).width($originalRow.eq(index).width());
        });
        return $helperRow;
}
```

20. In the *$("#peopleTable tbody").sortable()* method, pass a second option named *helper* and assign it a <u>reference</u> to the *fixHelper* function.

```
$("#peopleTable tbody").sortable({handle:"td.handle", helper: fixHelper});
```

21. Save your changes and browse *index.html*. The helper row should now appear with the same width as the original row being sorted.

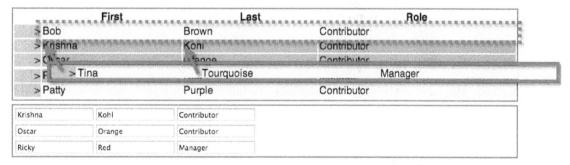

22. Close all project files.

Enhancing the user interface

Controlling page display

jQuery UI provides a set of three widgets for controlling content display.

Widgets	*Accordion*	Autocomplete	Button
	Datepicker	Dialog	*Menu*
	Progressbar	Slider	Spinner
	Tabs	Tooltip	

The user input and form widgets are discussed later in the course.

Understanding the general implementation approach

jQuery UI components consume an identified block of HTML markup, and replace it with the corresponding markup, styles, and code needed to render the visual widget.

While the specific source markup needed varies by control, generally the page display method is called on a jQuery object selected for the top-level element of a set of content.

```
<div id="title">Choose</div>
<div id="cities">
      <h3>Portland</h3>
      <div id="cities-1">
              <p>Ennui messenger bag tousled food truck readymade ...
...
</div>
// render a set of div blocks within an accordion display
$("#cities").accordion();
```

Creating a Menu

The jQuery UI *Menu* widget relies on one or more nested unordered lists of hyperlinked list items. A menu is created based on the list hierarchy. Clicking a menu item loads the corresponding page. Visual style depends on the theme chosen when building the jQuery library.

```
<ul id="cities" class="city-menu">
  <li> <a href="content/portland.html">Portland</a>
    <ul>
      <li><a href="content/portland.html#coffee">Coffee</a></li>
      <li><a href="content/portland.html#bookstores">Bookstores</a></li>
    </ul>
  </li>
...
$("#cities").menu();
```

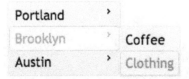

Configuring a menu and handling its events

The jQuery UI *Menu* API enables significant runtime control over menu behavior. Each time the user chooses a menu item, a *select* event is dispatched.

Options	disabled	icon	menus	position	role
Methods	blur	collapse	collapseAll	destroy	disable
	enable	expand	focus	isFirstItem	isLastItem
	next	nextPage	option	previous	previousPage
	refresh	select	widget		
Events	blur	create	focus	select	

http://api.jQueryUI.com/Menu/

Using Accordion display

The jQuery UI *Accordion* display controls the display of text embedded in nested *div* elements. Content may be embedded directly in the div elements. Alternately, *$.load()* requests targeting nested *div* elements could be made in response to Accordion *activate* events.

```
<div id="cities">
  <h3>Portland</h3>
    <div id="cities-1">
      <p>Ennui messenger bag tousled food truck readymade...</p>
    </div>
  <h3>Brooklyn</h3>
    <div id="cities-2">
      <p>High life flannel Austin, literally organic vice beard...</p>
    </div>
  <h3>Austin</h3>
    <div id="cities-3">
      <p>Locavore carles synth cliche twee. Semiotics lomo gastropub...</p>
    </div>
</div>
...
$("#cities").accordion();
```

Austin

> Portland

> Brooklyn

▾ Austin

Locavore carles synth cliche twee. Semiotics lomo gastropub, terry richardson organic neutra chambray. Meggings swag organic biodiesel, mlkshk try-hard godard pop-up typewriter banh mi aesthetic irony cray.

Configuring an accordion and handling its events

The jQuery UI *Accordion* API exposes a different underlying approach than a menu. Each time the user selects an accordion leaf, an *activate* event is dispatched.

Options	active	animate	collapsible	disabled	event
	header	heightStyle	icons		
Methods	destroy	disable	enable	option	refresh
	widget				
Events	activate	beforeActivate	create		

http://api.jQueryUI.com/Accordion/

Using Tabs display

The jQuery UI *Tabs* widget relies on a list of anchors with HREF values targeting either:

- embedded *div* elements with *id* corresponding to the anchor values

```
<div id="cities">
  <ul>
    <li><a href="#cities-1">Portland</a></li>
    <li><a href="#cities-2">Brooklyn</a></li>
    <li><a href="#cities-3">Austin</a></li>
  </ul>
  <div id="cities-1">
    <p>Ennui messenger bag tousled food truck readymade.
    ...
$("#cities").tabs();
```

- external files at the specified anchor URLs

```
<div id="cities">
  <ul>
    <li><a href="content/portland.html">Portland</a></li>
    <li><a href="content/brooklyn.html">Brooklyn</a></li>
    <li><a href="content/austin.html">Austin</a></li>
  </ul>
</div>
```

If external URLs are provided in the list, the external content is seamlessly loaded.

Locavore carles synth cliche twee. Semiotics lomo gastropub, terry richardson organic neutra chambray. Meggings swag organic biodiesel, mlkshk try-hard godard pop-up typewriter banh mi aesthetic irony cray. Lomo trust fund bespoke wes anderson occupy chambray, aesthetic banh mi intelligentsia. Iphone salvia high life put a bird on it. Vice actually forage tumblr, vegan

Configuring a tabs widget and handling its events

The jQuery UI *Tabs* widget provides a similar API to *Accordion*, but not identical. Notably, it exposes both *load* and *activate* events, to supports its built-in loading of external content. This behavior would require a bit more customization to support in an *Accordion*.

Options	active	collapsible	disabled	event	heightStyle
	hide	show			
Methods	destroy	disable	enable	load	option
	refresh	widget			
Events	activate	beforeActivate	beforeLoad	create	load

http://api.jQueryUI.com/Tabs/

Exercise: Implementing page control widgets

In this exercise you will configure markup for menu, tabs, and accordion display, handle related events, and access tab and panel data for displayed content.

After completion, you should be able to:

- Implement the Menu, Tabs, and Accordion widgets
- Use inline or external content for these widgets
- Respond to activation events on page control widgets
- Access header text and related menu, tab, and panel data

Steps

Review project files

1. Open the following project and review its starting files.

   `/ftjq/8-page-controls`

2. In *index.html*, notice four sections of commented markup:

   - *Menu from inline links*
   - *Accordion from inline text*
   - *Tabs from inline text*
   - *Tabs from external files*

Create a menu from inline text

3. Uncomment the *Menu from inline links* block of markup.

4. Review the structure to notice:

   - top level *div* with *id cities*
   - nested lists with with an anchor tag for each list item

5. In *js/script.js*, select the *cities div* and call the *.menu()* method on the jQuery object.

```
$(document).ready(function() {

    $("#cities").menu();
    ...
```

6. Save your changes and browse *index.html*. You should see the markup displayed as a two level menu, with links to pages in the */content* folder. Notice that the menu responds to keyboard input.

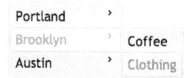

Note, actual appearance depends on the selected jQuery UI theme.

Create an accordion display from inline text

7. To prevent name collision, comment out the previous markup.

8. Uncomment the *Accordion from inline text* markup.

9. Review the structure to notice

   - *div* with *id title*

   - *div* with *id cities*, with alternating *h3* and *div* elements, each with paragraph content

10. In *js/script.js*, comment out the prior code creating the menu.

11. Select the new *cities div*, and call the *.accordion()* method on the jQuery object.

    ```
    // $("#cities").menu();
    $("#cities").accordion();
    ```

12. Save your changes and browse *index.html*. You should see the content *div* elements wrapped in accordion leaves named for the *h3* element prior to each *div*. Navigate through the accordion leaves.

Choose

▸ Portland

▸ Brooklyn

▾ Austin

Locavore carles synth cliche twee. Semiotics lomo gastropub, richardson organic neutra chambray. Meggings swag organic t mlkshk try-hard godard pop-up typewriter banh mi aesthetic

Access header text from an accordion activate event

13. In *js/script.js*, add an *accordionactivate* event *.on()* the *cities* element.

14. In the event handler, display the *.text()* of the *.newHeader* in the *ui* element passed into the function in the *title div*.

15. Your code should look like this:

```
$("#cities").accordion();
$("#cities").on("accordionactivate", function(event, ui){
    $("#title").text(ui.newHeader.text());
});
```

Note, time permitting, use this event to log and examine the ui object.

16. Save your changes and browse *index.html*. The *title div* should now update to display the header text of the selected accordion leaf.

High life flannel Austin, literally organic vice beard. PBR echo park cliche, portland seitan pitchfork locavore trust fund leggings. Irony keytar seitan,

Create a tab display from inline text

17. To prevent name collision, comment out the previous markup.

18. Uncomment the *Tabs from inline text* markup.

19. Review the markup to notice:

    * *div* with *id title*

    * top level *div* with *id cities*

    * list of links with anchors matching the *id* of *divs* below the list

20. In *js/script.js*, comment out the prior code creating the accordion.

21. Select the new *cities div*, and call the *.tabs()* method on the jQuery object.

22. Your code should look like this:

```
// $("#cities").accordion();
// $("#cities").on("accordionactivate", function(event, ui){
//     $("#title").text(ui.newHeader.text());
// });

$("#cities").tabs();
```

23. Save your changes and browse *index.html.* You should see the *div* content separated into tabs named for the *li* elements in the markup.

Ennui messenger bag tousled food truck readymade. Cosby sweater 8-bit shoreditch, retro street art etsy thundercats kale chips semiotics skateboard bespoke. Biodiesel farm-to-table terry richardson, umami next level vegan scenester PBR. VHS blog beard, cliche carles mixtape aesthetic letterpress tonx

Access tab text from a tabs activate event

24. In *js/script.js,* create a *tabsactivate* event handler *.on()* the *cities* element.

25. In the event handler, assign the *.text()* of the *.newTab* of the *ui* object to the *title div.*

26. Your code should look like this:

```
$("#cities").tabs();
$("#cities").on("tabsactivate", function(event, ui){
    $("#title").text(ui.newTab.text());
});
```

Note, time permitting, use this event to log and examine the ui object.

27. Save your changes and browse *index.html.* The title should now update to match the selected tab.

Locavore carles synth cliche twee. Semiotics lomo gastropub, terry richardson organic neutra chambray. Meggings swag organic biodiesel, mlkshk try-hard godard pop-up typewriter banh mi aesthetic irony cray. Lomo trust fund bespoke wes anderson occupy chambray, aesthetic banh mi intelligentsia. Iphone salvia high life put a bird on it. Vice actually forage tumblr, vegan

Create a tab display from externally loaded files

28. To prevent name collision, comment out the previous markup.

29. Uncomment the *Tabs from external files* markup.

30. Review the new markup to notice:

    - *div* with *id title*

    - top level *div* with *id cities*

    - list of items with anchors referencing external files

    - nothing else

31. Save your changes and browse *index.html*. There should be no change from the previous display, because jQuery UI Tabs automatically loads the referenced pages.

32. Close the project files.

Summary

In this unit you have learned:

- jQuery plugins are extensions to the prototype jQuery function

- jQuery UI is a plugin (library) providing widgets, interactions, and effects based on a common core

- *jQueryUI.com/Download* enables download of selectively configured, themed libraries

- Both CSS and JS files must be attached to a page, to use jQuery UI elements

- jQuery UI themes may be selected, or customized using jQuery UI Themeroller

- Interactions enable selection, sorting, dragging, dropping, and resizing of elements

- Interaction events provide a *ui* argument providing access to impacted elements

- All jQuery UI widgets, interactions, and effects expose various options, methods, and events specific to the particular element

- There are inconsistencies in event naming (e.g., "selectableselected" vs "sort")

- jQuery UI elements are each configure by options, commonly specified by an inline object passed to the enabling UI method

- jQuery UI widgets select HTML markup in specified formats and re-render the content using themed Accordion, Tabs, and Menu page controls

Review

1. You are using both the *draggable* and *selectable* interactions. You want to drag an element without selecting it. How could do this?

2. You want each element *selected* by the user to be added to a shopping cart *div*. Would you need to use a *$.each()* loop in the event handler to access the selected items?

3. You receive feedback that users are accidentally selecting items in a list, without meaning to. How could you improve the user's experience?

4. You need to provide a structured way to display a set of 5 continually updated text documents. How could you do this with minimal code?

5. You want to display the title of the previously selected tab in the panel of the newly selected tab. How could you do this?

Unit 9
Using jQuery UI with form-based input

Objectives

After completing this unit, you should understand:

- Implementing *Autocomplete*, *Datepicker*, *Slider*, *Button*, and *Dialog* widgets

- Configuring jQuery UI Widget *options*, *methods*, and *events*

- Internationalizing a *Datepicker*

- Loading and configuring external data to support an *Autocomplete* widget

- Using *Slider* widgets to capture individual or ranged values

- Creating *Button* widgets to integrate basic *input* elements with a jQuery UI theme

- Conditionally displaying *form* elements by *div* or *Dialog*

Improving user input with jQuery UI widgets

Surveying the available widgets

Distinct from the content organizing widgets - Accordion, Tabs, and Menu - are the widgets commonly used to capture data in forms, though they are not necessarily restricted to forms. For example, a set of Slider widgets could be used to modify color values for another element.

Widgets are implemented sufficiently similarly that learning some of them will enable you to easily learn and use the rest. The highlighted widgets will be discussed in detail.

Widgets	Accordion	**Autocomplete**	**Button**
	Datepicker	**Dialog**	Menu
	Progressbar	**Slider**	Spinner
	Tabs	Tooltip	

Documentation for all widgets can be found at:

http://API.jQueryUI.com/category/Widgets/

Demos for each widget can be found at:

http://www.jQueryUI.com/*widgetname*

Understanding the general implementation approach

Like jQuery UI Interactions, Widgets are implemented by calling a method named for the widget on a selected element. The element may be an *input* or *div*, depending on whether an editable *input* field is inherent to the widget's behavior.

```
$(selector).widgetname();
```

Setting jQuery UI Widget options

If non-default behavior is needed, a configuration object is passed to the method. The properties of this object may represent *options* or *events* related to the widget.

```
$(selector).widgetMethod({option:value, event:function() {...}, ...});
```

The object may be passed inline, as shown above, or separately created.

```
var config = {};
config.option = value;
config.event = function(event, ui) { ... };
$(selector).widgetname(config);
```

Calling jQuery UI Widget methods

jQuery UI Widget methods are not called directly on the selected jQuery object. Instead, they are called by passing the method name to the widget function itself, called on the selected object. If the method takes parameters, they are passed subsequent to the method name.

For example, to call the open method of a jQuery UI Dialog widget:

```
<div id="box">
        <p>Let's have some dialog about this ...</p>
</div>
<button id="button">Open Dialog</button>
...
// render box as a dialog box
$("#box").dialog({autoOpen:false});

// open the dialog box
$("#button").dialog("open"); // not $("#button").open();
```

Using the Autocomplete widget

The Autocomplete widget suggests terms, from an array assigned as its *source* option, as the user types into a selected text *input*.

```
var books = ["Dracula", "Frankenstein", "Walden"];
$("#title").autocomplete({source:books});
...
<input id="title" />
```

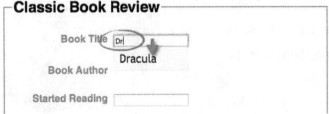

Using an object array with Autocomplete

The source may be a simple string array, or an object array. If it is an object array, the objects must include label and value properties.

label   displayed in the Autocomplete menu

value   assigned to the text input when corresponding label selected

If only a *label* is provided in the *source* object array, it is used as both *label* and *value*.

```
[
        { "title": "Les Misérables", "author" : "Victor Hugo" },
        { "title": "Ulysses", "author" : "James Joyce" },
...
var books = [];
$.getJSON("data/no-copyright-books.json", function(data){
        $.each(data, function(index, item){
                // create objects for use by autocomplete field
                item.label = item.title;
                item.value = item.author;
                // add configured item to books array
                books.push(item);
        });
});
$("#title").autocomplete({source:books});
```

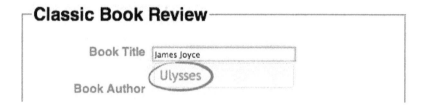

Surveying the API

Options	appendTo	autoFocus	delay	disabled
	minLength	position	source	
Methods	close	destroy	disable	enable
	option	search	widget	
Events	change	close	create	focus
	open	response	search	select

Details of each are available at:

http://API.jQueryUI.com/Autocomplete/

Handling Autocomplete events

Events are handled by assigning a function to the event name in the Autocomplete configuration object. Like other jQuery UI event handlers, both *event* and *ui* arguments are passed.

event   standard event object with type, target, and related properties

ui   for Autocomplete, *ui.item* refers to the source object for the selected label

```
[
        { "title": "Les Misérables", "author" : "Victor Hugo" },
        { "title": "Ulysses", "author" : "James Joyce" },
...
$("#title").autocomplete({
        // assign books array as the autocomplete source
        source: books,
        // handle select events by displaying author name
        select: function(event, ui){
                $("#author").text(ui.item.author);
        }
});
```

┌─**Classic Book Review**─────────────────────

      Book Title   `Grimm's Fairy Tales|`

      Book Author   Jacob Grimm and Wilhelm Grimm

Exercise: Implementing jQuery UI Autocomplete

In this exercise you will implement an autocomplete field using a simple embedded array, then an externally loaded array. You will then use an event to take data related to the selected item and display it in a different field.

After completion, you should be able to:

- Implement a jQuery UI *Autocomplete* widget

- Understand the *label* and *value* properties used by the widget

- Handle *Autocomplete* select events

- Access *Autocomplete* data related to a selection for use in other fields

Steps

Review project files

1. Open the following project and review its starting files.

   `/ftjq/9-autocomplete`

2. Browse *index.html* and notice:

   - in the form, text fields are placeholders for jQuery UI elements to be added

   - untyped and unnamed *input* element with *id title*

   - *span* element with *id author*

   - a full (all interactions, widgets, and effects) version of jQuery UI 1.10 with related libraries and CSS is linked to the page, with the default *ui-lightness* theme

Implement basic autocompletion

3. In *js/script.js*, declare an *Array books* with three values: *Dracula*, *Frankenstein*, and *Walden*.

4. Assign the *books* array as the *source* value of an inline options object passed to the *.autocomplete()* method called on the *title* field in the form.

5. Your code should look like this:

```
$(document).ready(function() {

    var books = ["Dracula", "Frankenstein", "Walden"];
    $("#title").autocomplete({source:books});
    ...
```

6. Save your changes and browse *index.html*. Type the first two letters of any of the three book titles in the title field, and an autocomplete menu should appear.

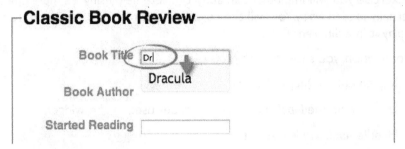

Load and configure external JSON for use by Autocomplete widget

7. Comment out the two previous lines of code.

8. Open and review *data/no-copyright-books.json* to notice the *title* and *author* properties of each object in the array.

```
script.js          ×    index.html        ×    no-copyright-books.json ×
 1  [
 2
 3  { "title": "Les Misérables", "author" : "Victor Hugo" },
 4  { "title": "Adventures of Huckleberry Finn", "author" : "Mark Twain" },
 5  { "title": "Pride and Prejudice", "author" : "Jane Austen" },
 6  { "title": "The Adventures of Sherlock Holmes", "author" : "Sir Arthur Conan Doyle" },
 7  { "title": "Grimm's Fairy Tales", "author" : "Jacob Grimm and Wilhelm Grimm" },
 8  { "title": "Beowulf", "author": "Unknown" },
 9  { "title": "Leaves of Grass", "author" : "Walt Whitman" },
10  { "title": "The Prince", "author" : "Niccolò Machiavelli" },
11  { "title": "The Divine Comedy", "author" : "Dante, Illustrated", "author" : "Dante Alighieri" },
```

9. In *js/script.js*, declare an empty array *books*.

10. Load *data/no-copyright-books.json* into the page.

11. Loop over *.each()* item in the data.

12. In the loop assign a new property *label* to *item* with the *title* value of the current *item*.

13. Assign a new property *value* to *item* with the *author* value of the current *item*.

14. Use the *.push()* method to add this *item* to the *books* array.

15. Following the loop, *log* the books array to the *console*.

16. Your code should look like this:

```
var books = [];

$.getJSON("data/no-copyright-books.json", function(data){
     $.each(data, function(index, item){
          item.label = item.title;
          item.value = item.author;
          books.push(item);
     });
     console.log(books);
});
```

17. Save your changes and browse *index.html*. Open your browser console, and verify *books* is populated as an array of objects with *label*, *value*, *title*, and *author* properties.

```
▼ 0: Object
    author: "Victor Hugo"
    label: "Les Misérables"
    title: "Les Misérables"
    value: "Victor Hugo"
  ▶ __proto__: Object
  ▶ 1: Object
  ▶ 2: Object
```

Implement external data for autocomplete

18. In *js/script.js*, after the declaration of the books array, assign the *books* array as the *source* for the *title* autocomplete field.

```
var books = [];

$("#title").autocomplete({source:books});

$.getJSON("data/no-copyright-books.json", function(data){
    ...
```

19. Save your changes and browse *index.html*. Type letters in the *Book Title* field and an autocomplete menu should appear. Use the down arrow to move across items, and notice the author appears in the title field. Select a title, and the menu should close.

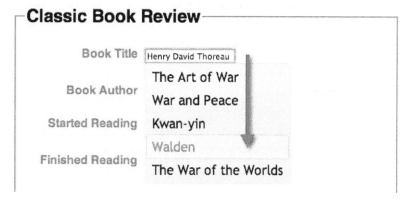

Implement select event handler to populate author field

20. In *js/script.js*, in the *$.getJSON()* method, comment out the line assigning *author* as the *value* property of the *item* object.

21. Also, comment out the *log* statement.

```
$.getJSON("data/no-copyright-books.json", function(data){
    $.each(data, function(index, item){
        item.label = item.title;
        // item.value = item.author;
        books.push(item);
    });
    // console.log(books);
});
```

22. In the *.autocomplete()* method, add a *select* property to the *options* object, and assign an inline *function* with *event* and *ui* arguments, to handle *select* events from the *title* field.

23. In the event handler, *log* the *ui* object.

24. Assign the the *author* property of *ui.item* as *.text()* for the author field.

    Note, why wouldn't you display the value property here?

25. Your code should look like this:

```
$("#title").autocomplete({
                    source: books,
                    select: function(event, ui){
                        console.log(ui);
                        $("#author").text(ui.item.author);
                    }
});
```

26. Save your changes and browse *index.html*. Open your browser console. Type letters in the title field, and select a book title. The title field should populate with the book title, and the author field with the author name. In the console, notice that in the absence of an explicitly set value property, one is created with the same value assigned as title.

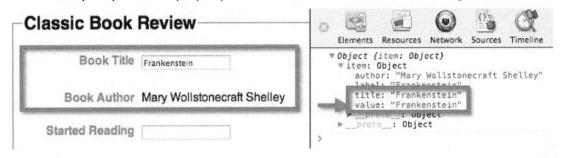

27. Close all project files.

Using the Datepicker widget

By default, the Datepicker widget displays a calendar when focus enters its text *input*. When a date is selected, its value is written back into the text *input*.

```
<input name="reviewdate" />
...
$("input[name='reviewdate']").datepicker();
```

Surveying the API

The Datepicker API uses slightly different naming conventions, and is more extensive, than the API of other widgets. This is only a partial list.

Options	buttonImage	changeMonth	dateFormat	defaultDate
	maxDate	minDate	numberOfMonths	(more ...)
Methods	dialog	hide	show	getDate
	setDate	option	widget	
Events	beforeShow	beforeShowDay	onChangeMoYr	onClose
	onSelect			

Details of each are available at:

http://API.jQueryUI.com/Datepicker/

Controlling date format

The resulting date format is controlled by passing a format string to the dateFormat option.

```
<input name="reviewdate" />
...
$("input[name*='date']").datepicker({dateFormat:"mm-dd-yy"});
```

Internationalizing the Datepicker

Introducing jQuery UI language configuration

Internationalization ("i18n") can be applied to the Datepicker by assigning an object configured with localized month name and similar properties, to a language code assigned to the *regional* property of the Datepicker.

```
/* Dutch (UTF-8) initialisation for the jQuery UI date picker plugin. */
/* Written by Mathias Bynens <http://mathiasbynens.be/> */
jQuery(function($){
$.datepicker.regional.nl = {
  ...
  currentText: 'Vandaag',
  monthNames: ['januari', 'februari', 'maart', 'april', 'mei', 'juni',
'juli', 'augustus', 'september', 'oktober', 'november', 'december'],
  monthNamesShort: ['jan', 'feb', 'mrt', 'apr', 'mei', 'jun',
'jul', 'aug', 'sep', 'okt', 'nov', 'dec'],
  ...};
  $.datepicker.setDefaults($.datepicker.regional['nl']);
});
```

Currently, these configurations are specific to the Datepicker widget. Fortunately, the configurations for about 100 languages are freely available as individual files, or a single comprehensive file, in regular or minified text.

List of individual Datepicker i18n files:

http://jquery-ui.googlecode.com/svn/tags/latest/ui/i18n/

Comprehensive, minified file:

http://jquery-ui.googlecode.com/svn/tags/latest/ui/minified/i18n/jquery-ui-i18n.min.js

Implementing Datepicker i18n

To implement Datepicker i18n you:

1. Include the relevant i18n files in your page

```
<script type="text/javascript" src="js/jquery-ui-i18n.min.js"></script>
```

2. Set the default language from the regional configuration objects (empty string is English)

```
$.datepicker.setDefaults($.datepicker.regional[""]);
```

3. In a relevant way for the project, select a language specific configuration object

```
var languageCode = "es";
var languageConfigObject = $.datepicker.regional[languageCode];
```

4. Pass the configuration object to the Datepicker

```
$("input[name='reviewdate']").datepicker(languageConfigObject);
```

Configuring multiple Datepickers to select related dates

Introducing the options and events

Options and events can be used to create related behavior between Datepickers. For example, the following could be used to configure related start date and end date widgets.

defaultDate	sets initially selected date (default is current date in browser)
changeMonth	displays drop down to choose month (default is off)
numberOfMonths	specify how many months to display together
minDate / maxDate	set earliest and latest selectable dates
onClose	event when Datepicker closes, is passed the selectedDate

Implementing related Datepickers

These options and events could be implemented as:

```
$("input[name='startdate']").datepicker({
 // set initial display
 defaultDate: "-1w", changeMonth: true, numberOfMonths: 2,
 // set minimum date of finishdate based on this selected date
 onClose: function(selectedDate) {
  $("input[name='finishdate']").datepicker("option", "minDate", selectedDate);
 }
});

$("input[name='finishdate']").datepicker({
 // set initial display
 changeMonth: true, numberOfMonths: 2,
 // set maximum date of stardate based on this selected date
 onClose: function(selectedDate) {
  $("input[name='startdate']").datepicker("option", "maxDate", selectedDate);
 }
});
```

Exercise: Implementing jQuery UI Datepicker

In this exercise you will create and configure three Datepicker widgets, internationalize them, and configure two of them for multiple month display with date range coordination.

After completion, you should be able to:

- Implement a jQuery UI Datepicker widget

- Locate and implement a jQuery UI Datepicker internationalization ("i18n") file

- Configure display options for Datepicker widgets

- Implement event handlers to coordinate ranged date selection between two widgets

Steps

Review project files

1. Open the following project and review its starting files.

   `/ftjq/9-datepicker`

2. Browse *index.html* and notice:

   - in the form, text fields are placeholders for jQuery UI elements to be added

   - *input* elements *startdate*, *finishdate*, and *reviewdate*

3. Notice the minified file *jquery-ui-i18n.min.js* has been added to *ljs*.

Implement and configure Datepicker for all date fields

4. In *js/script.js*, select all *input* elements which include the word *date* in their name, and call the *.datepicker()* method on them to render these fields as this widget type.

```
$(document).ready(function() {

    $("input[name*='date']").datepicker();
    ...
```

5. Save your changes and browse *index.html*. When you select any of the three date fields you should see a *Datepicker* appear. The widgets appear in the *ui-lightness* theme chosen for the pre-included jQuery UI library.

6. In *js/script.js*, modify the *.datepicker()* method to use an inline options object to assign the *dateFormat* property using *dd-mm-yy* as the format string.

```
$("input[name*='date']").datepicker({dateFormat:"mm-dd-yy"});
```

7. Save your changes and browse *index.html*. Select a date in any date field. You should see the default *mm/dd/yy* (slash separator) format modified to *mm-dd-yy* (dash separator).

Internationalize Datepicker dipslay

8. In *index.html*, use a *script* element to include the *js/jquery-ui-i18n.min.js* file after the jQuery libraries and prior to the project *script.js* file.

```
<script type="text/javascript"
        src="js/jquery-ui-1.10.0.custom/js/jquery-1.9.0.js"></script>
<script type="text/javascript"
        src="js/jquery-ui-1.10.0.custom/js/jquery-ui-1.10.0.custom.js"></script>
<script type="text/javascript" src="js/jquery-ui-i18n.min.js"></script>
<script type="text/javascript" src="js/script.js"></script>
```

Note, this file can be accessed from the Google CDN at this URL
http://jquery-ui.googlecode.com/svn/tags/latest/ui/minified/i18n/jquery-ui-i18n.min.js

9. In *js/script.js*, above the *.datepicker()* assignment, use the empty string to assign the default *regional* code (English) to the datepicker.

```
$.datepicker.setDefaults($.datepicker.regional[""]);
$("input[name*='date']").datepicker({dateFormat:"mm-dd-yy"});
```

10. Assign a new local variable *languageCode* the string value *es*.

11. In the *.datepicker()* method, use *languageCode* to reference and assign a regional format object as the first argument to this method, followed by the existing options object.

12. Your code should look like this:

```
$.datepicker.setDefaults($.datepicker.regional[""]);
var languageCode = "es";
$("input[name*='date']").datepicker($.datepicker.regional[languageCode],
        {dateFormat:"mm-dd-yy"});
```

Note, if you do not set the default region, as shown, and no other language is assigned, the Datepicker will display the first language configured in the localization script included in index.html.

13. Save your changes and browse *index.html*. Select a date. Each of the three datepickers should now display in Spanish.

Configure multiple month display

14. In *js/script.js*, <u>comment out</u> the existing *.datepicker()* statement.

15. Select and configure a separate *.datepicker()* each for *stardate*, *finishdate*, and *reviewdate*.

16. With *startdate* and *finishdate*, use an inline options object to assign *changeMonth* as *true*, and *numberOfMonths* as *2*, for both widgets.

Note, for speed, write the stardate statement, duplicate it, and change the selector to finishdate.

17. Your code should look like this:

```
// $("input[name*='date']").datepicker($.datepicker.regional[languageCode],
{dateFormat:"mm-dd-yy"});

$("input[name='reviewdate']").datepicker();
$("input[name='startdate']").datepicker({
                              changeMonth: true,
                              numberOfMonths: 2
                              });
$("input[name='finishdate']").datepicker({
                              changeMonth: true,
                              numberOfMonths: 2
                              });
```

18. Save your changes and browse *index.html*. Select a *startdate* or *finishdate*. You should see two months appear, and the first should display a *changeMonth* combo box. You can navigate between months by keyboard, arrow icons, or combo box.

Use events to configure date range display between two datepickers

19. In *js/script.js*, in the options objects for *stardate*, add an *onClose* event handler *function* which receives one argument *selectedDate*.

20. In this event handler, select and configure the *minDate* option of the *finishdate* datepicker with the *selectedDate* value.

21. Your code should look like this:

```
$("input[name='startdate']").datepicker({
        changeMonth: true,
        numberOfMonths: 3,
        onClose: function(selectedDate) {
                $("input[name='finishdate']").datepicker("option",
                        "minDate", selectedDate);
        }
});
```

22. Duplicate this entire statement, paste it below itself, and modify the *finishdate*, *startdate*, and *maxDate* assignments, as shown.

```
$("input[name='finishdate']").datepicker({
        changeMonth: true,
        numberOfMonths: 3,
        onClose: function(selectedDate) {
                $("input[name='startdate']").datepicker("option",
                        "maxDate", selectedDate);
        }
});
```

23. In the *startdate* datepicker, add an option of *-1w* to set the *defaultDate* to one week prior to the default (current) date.

```
$("input[name='startdate']").datepicker({
    defaultDate: "-1w",
    changeMonth: true,
    numberOfMonths: 3,
    onClose: function(selectedDate) {
        $("input[name='finishdate']").datepicker("option",
            "minDate", selectedDate);
    }
});
```

24. Save your changes and browse *index.html*. Select a *startdate*, then select a *finishdate*. The default *startdate* should be one week prior to the current date, and the *finishdate* should be restricted to no earlier than the *startdate*.

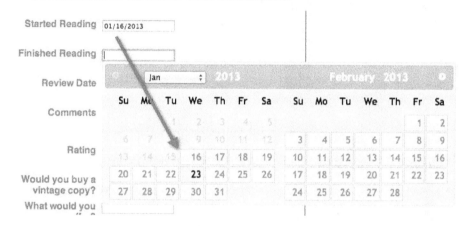

25. Close all project files.

Using the Slider and Button widgets

Using the Slider widget

The Slider widget provides one or more handles along a horizontal or vertical bar, each of which represent a point along a range of values specified for the bar. The handles may be dragged, or the bar may be clicked to move the handle. Events are used to capture the value represented by a handle's position at any given point in time.

Because the Slider itself does not accept input, it is commonly configured using a *div* element.

```
<label>Rating</label>
<div id="rating"></div>
...
$("#rating").slider();
```

Rating

Surveying the API

Options	animate	disabled	max	min
	orientation	range	step	value
	values			
Methods	destroy	disable	enable	option
	value	values	widget	
Events	create	start	slide	change
	stop			

Details of each are available at:

http://API.jQueryUI.com/Slider/

Configuring a Slider and displaying its values

Options and events can be used to set the range and visual behavior for a Slider, as well as to update an external display element.

animate	whether and how quickly to animate the motion along the slider
value	initial or assigned value of a single value slider
range	whether slider represents a range (true) or single value (false, default)
values	an array of initial or assigned values for a range slider
min / max	the low and high values supported by the slider
step	the amount of change between each point along the min to max range
slide	event dispatched with event and ui arguments as handler moves each step
ui.value	property representing currently moving handle's value
ui.values[0 ... n]	array referencing the current value of each handle of a multi-value slider

A Slider does not inherently display its values as text. The *values* property defines the number of handles. The *ui.values* array holds and updates one value per handle.

```
<span id="offer"></span>
...
$("#offer").text("$10 - $150");
$("#offerslider").slider({
      range: true,
      min: 1, max: 250, values: [10, 150], step: 1,
      // display low/high range values as text in offer span
      slide: function(event, ui) {
            $("#offer").text("$" + ui.values[0] + " - " + "$" + ui.values[1]);
      }
});
```

Would you buy a ☐
vintage copy?

What would you $23 - $111
offer?

Using the Button / Buttonset widgets

The Button widget converts *button, anchor, button input, radio input,* and *checkbox input* elements or element sets into themed buttons with appropriate hover and active styles.

Options	disabled	icons	label	text
Methods	destroy	disable	enable	refresh
	option	widget		
Events	create			

Details of each are available at:

http://API.jQueryUI.com/Button/

Elements configured as themed buttons still respond as their underlying element. So, themed *button* elements still dispatch *click* events. *Radio input* elements assigned a *name* and *value* will post that value in form submission, etc.

Creating a single themed button

A basic button element can be replaced with a button matching the theme chosen for the particular jQuery UI library loaded to the page.

```
<button id="submit">Submit</button>
...
$("#submit").button();
```

```
                              Submit
```

Creating a themed toggle button set

Radio input sets can be rendered as toggle buttons. A *label* must be provided for each radio input to specify its text. A *value* must be provided if the elements are to be submitted by a form.

```
<label class="field" for="condition">Book condition</label>
<div id="conditionbuttonset">
  <input id="condition1" type="radio" name="condition" value="Good" />
    <label for="condition1">Good</label>
  <input id="condition2" type="radio" name="condition" value="Fine" />
    <label for="condition2">Fine</label>
  <input id="condition3" type="radio" name="condition" value="Mint"
      checked="checked" />
    <label for="condition3">Mint</label>
</div>
...
$("#conditionbuttonset").buttonset();
```

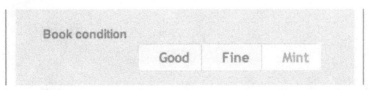

Exercise: Implementing jQuery UI Slider and Button

In this exercise you will create a slider visually displaying a rating value, a slider displaying a range of two values as text, an alternatively displayed radio button set, and a toggle to show and hide a form section.

After completion, you should be able to:

- Implement a jQuery UI *Slider* and *Button*

- Configure a *Slider* for *min*, *max*, *default*, and *range* values

- Handle *slide* events to display current Slider *values* as custom graphics or text

- Display a radio button set as a button bar

- Change visibility of a form section in response to user input

Steps

Review project files

1. Open the following project and review its starting files.

   ```
   /ftjq/9-slider-button
   ```

2. In *js/script.js* notice pre-built *showStars($target, number)* function, which appends a specified *number* of star graphics to *$target*.

3. In */images*, notice new graphic *star.png*.

4. In *css/style.css*, pre-defined styles for *ratingslider*, *offerslider*, *conditionbuttonset*, and *offerwidgets*.

Implement slider with graphic display

5. In *index.html*, comment out or delete the existing *rating input*, and replace it with a *span* with *id rating*, and a *div* with *id ratingslider*.

```
<p>
    <label class="field" for="rating">Rating</label>
    <!-- <input name="rating" type="" /> -->
    <span id="rating"></span>
    <div id="ratingslider"></div>
</p>
```

6. In *js/script.js*, declare a *var defaultRating* with the value *5*.

7. Select and call the *.slider()* method on *ratingslider*, and configure it with the following options:

- *animate: "slow"*

- *value: defaultRating*

- *min: I*

- *max: 7*

- *step: I*

8. Your code should look like this:

```
var defaultRating = 5;
$("#ratingslider").slider({
                    animate: "slow",
                    value: defaultRating,
                    min: 1,
                    max: 7,
                    step: 1
                    });
```

9. Save your changes and browse *index.html.* You should see a slider which navigates among 7 steps. Click on the slider, not the button, to see the animation.

Use event to display slider output

10. In *js/script.js*, assign a *function* to handle *event* and *ui* arguments to the *slide* option of the *ratingslider*.

11. In this event handler, pass a selector for the *rating span* to the *showStars($target, number)* function, along with the *value* property of the *ui* argument.

12. Immediately following the *defaultRating* variable, call the *showStars($target, number)* function, and pass it a *rating* field selector, along with the *defaultValue* variable.

13. Your code should look like this:

```
var defaultRating = 5;
showStars($("#rating"), defaultRating);
$("#ratingslider").slider({
                    animate: "slow",
                    value: defaultRating,
                    min: 1,
                    max: 7,
                    step: 1,
                    slide: function(event, ui) {
                            showStars($("#rating"), ui.value);
                    }
                    });
```

14. Save your changes and browse *index.html*. Move the *ratingslider*, and you should see stars appear to display the current *ratingslider* value.

Display ranged values using slider

15. In *index.html*, comment out or delete the existing *offer input*, and replace it with a *span* with *id offer*, and a *div* with *id offerslider*.

```
<p>
    <label class="field" for="offer">What would you offer?</label>
    <!-- <input name="offer" type="" /> -->
    <span id="offer"></span>
    <div id="offerslider"></div>
</p>
```

16. In *js/script.js*, select and call the *.slider()* method on *offerslider*, and configure it with the following options:

    * *range: true*

    * *min: 1*

    * *max: 250*

    * *values: [10, 150]*

    * *step: 1*

17. Configure the *slide* option with a UI event handling *function*.

18. In the event handler, display the first and second values in the *ui.values* array as *.text()* in the *offer span*, surrounded by relevant "$" and " - " display strings.

19. Above the *.slider()* method, select the *offer span* and set its initial *.text()* as *$10 - $150*.

20. Your code should look like this:

```
$("#offer").text("$10 - $150");
$("#offerslider").slider({
                  range: true,
                  min: 1,
                  max: 250,
                  values: [10, 150],
                  step: 1,
                  slide: function(event, ui) {
      $("#offer").text("$" + ui.values[0] + " - " + "$" + ui.values[1]);
                  }
                  });
```

21. Save your changes and browse *index.html*. You should see a ranged slider, which updates a displayed offer range when the handles are moved.

Configure alternative radio button display

22. In *index.html*, above the *p* element containing *offer* and *offerslider*, add a new *p* element containing *label* element with *class field*, containing the text *Book condition*.

```
<p>
        <label class="field">Book condition</label>
</p>
<p>
        <label class="field" for="offer">Offer range</label>
        <span id="offer"></span>
        ...
```

23. Below the new *label*, add a *div conditionbuttonset*.

24. In the new *div*, add an *input* of *type radio* with *name condition* and *id condition1*, followed by a *label* element for *condition1*, surrounding the value *Good*.

25. Duplicate this *input*, modifying it with *id condition2* and *value Fine*, and the next as *id condition3* and value *Mint*.

26. Set the *checked* attribute of *input id condition3* as *checked*.

27. Your code should look like this:

```
<p>
  <label class="field" for="condition">Book condition</label>
  <div id="conditionbuttonset">
    <input id="condition1" type="radio" name="condition"/>
      <label for="condition1">Good</label>

    <input id="condition2" type="radio" name="condition"/>
      <label for="condition2">Fine</label>

    <input id="condition3" type="radio"  name="condition" checked="checked" />
      <label for="condition3">Mint</label>
  </div>
</p>
```

28. In *js/script.js*, select and call the *.buttonset()* method on *conditionbuttonset*.

```
$("#conditionbuttonset").buttonset();
```

29. Select and call the *.button()* method on the *submit* button.

```
$("#submit").button();
```

30. Save your changes and browse *index.html*. You should see a button set as shown:

Selectively display a form section

31. In *index.html*, surround the *p* elements for the *condition* and *offer* widgets with a new *div* with *id offerwidgets*.

```
<div id="offerwidgets">
  <p>
    <label class="field" for="condition">Book condition</label>
    <div id="conditionbuttonset">
      ...
      ...
    <span id="offer"></span>
    <div id="offerslider"></div>
  </p>
</div>
```

32. In *js/script.js*, write a *click* event handler for the *checkbox input* element with *name buy*.

33. In this event handler, select and call the *.toggle()* method on *offerwidgets*.

34. Above the event handler, select and call the *.hide()* method on *offerwidgets*.

35. Your code should look like this:

```
$("#offerwidgets").hide();
$("input[name='buy']").on("click", function(event){
    $("#offerwidgets").toggle();
});
```

36. Save your changes and browse *index.html*. The widgets related to making an offer to buy a vintage copy of the book should be initially hidden, and display when the *Would you like to buy a vintage copy?* checkbox is clicked.

Note, the background color is set by pre-built CSS for the offerwidgets id

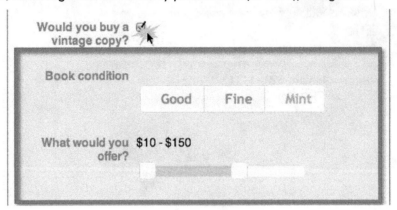

37. Close all project files.

Using the Dialog widget

The Dialog widget displays the contents of a specified div element as a pop up dialog box. It supports visual features including:

- modal (block other input) or non-modal

- draggable

- resizable

- button or button set

- close button

```
<div id="contactdialog">
    <fieldset>
        <legend>Contact Information</legend>
        <label class="field" for="offeraddress">Email Address</label>
        <input name="email" type="text" class="email" />
    </fieldset>
</div>
...
$("#contactdialog").dialog();
```

Surveying the API

Options	appendTo	autoOpen	buttons	closeOnEsc	closeText
	dialogClass	draggable	height	hide	maxHeight
	maxWidth	minHeight	minWidth	modal	position
	resizable	show	title	width	
Methods	close	destroy	isOpen	moveToTop	open
	option	widget			
Events	beforeClose	create	open	focus	dragStart
	drag	dragStop	resizeStart	resize	resizeStop
	close				

Details of each are available at:

http://API.jQueryUI.com/Dialog/

Configuring and opening Dialog widget

The Dialog widget is broadly configurable. Some key options and events include:

autoOpen whether Dialog opens as the page loads (defaults to true)

width / height defaults to fit content and can be adjusted

modal whether the background is disabled while Dialog is open (default to false)

open jQuery UI method called - as *.dialog("open")* - to open the Dialog box

```
<button id="contactbutton">Add Contact Information</button>
<div id="contactdialog">
      <fieldset>
            <legend>Contact Information</legend>
            <label class="field" for="offeraddress">Email Address</label>
            <input name="email" type="text" class="email" />
      </fieldset>
</div>
...
$("#contactdialog").dialog({
      autoOpen: false, width:500, modal: true
});

$("#contactbutton").on("click", function(event){
      $("#contactdialog").dialog("open");
});
```

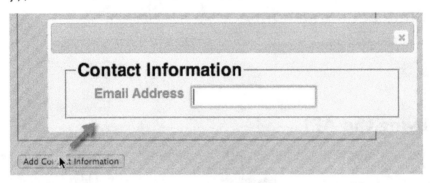

Adding buttons to a Dialog widget

Buttons are added to a Dialog by providing configuration objects to the *buttons* array of the Dialog. These objects support a *text* property to assign the button text, and a *click* property to assign a *click* event handler *function* for the button.

buttons   array of button configuration objects with *text* and *click* handler

```
$("#contactdialog").dialog({
  autoOpen: false,
  width:500,
  modal: true,
  buttons: [
    {text: "Close", click: function(event){$(this).dialog("close")}},
    {text: "Clear", click: function(event){$("input[name='email']").val("")}}
  ]
});
```

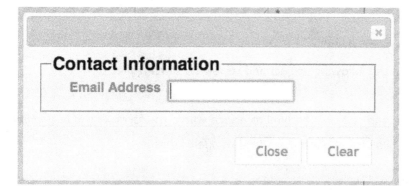

Exercise: Implementing jQuery UI Dialog

In this exercise you will conditionally display a dialog to gather an email address if the user wishes to be sent vintage book offers. The dialog will display buttons allowing the user to choose whether to provide an email address or not.

After completion, you should be able to:

- Implement a jQuery UI *Dialog* widget

- Configure a dialog widget for size, default open state, and modal status

- Control opening and closing of the dialog widget

- Display dialog buttons and handle their events

Steps

Review project files

1. Open the following project and review its starting files.

   `/ftjq/9-dialog`

2. Open and review *index.html* to notice within the form with *id reviewform*:

   - *span* with *id offeremail* added to *offerwidgets div*

```
<p>
  <span id="offeremail"></span>
</p>
```

   - *div* with *id offerdialog* with additional fields

```
<div id="offerdialog">
  <fieldset>
    <legend>Contact me with offers</legend>
    <label class="field" for="offeraddress">Email Address</label>
    <input id="email" name="email" type="text" />
  </fieldset>
</div>
```

3. Browse *index.html*. Notice the *offerdialog div* is displayed.

Would you buy a ☐
vintage copy?
┌─**Contact me with offers**───────────
│ Email Address [   ]
└──────────────────────────────────────

[Submit]

Create dialog from page div

4. In *js/script.js*, select the *offerdialog* element and call the *.dialog()* method.

```
$("#offerdialog").dialog();
```

5. Save your changes and browse *index.html*. The *offerdialog div* should disappear from the page, and now display as a non-model dialog. Drag the dialog from its top bar. Close the dialog using the top-right close button.

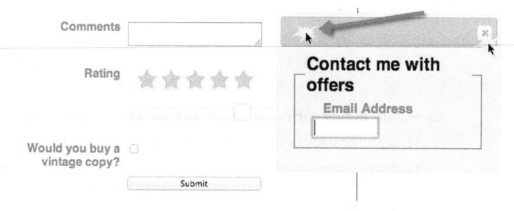

Note, recall that Dialog default appearance, like all widgets, is determined by the theme chosen when downloading the jQuery UI library. Pre-built alternatives can be chosen and custom themes created.

Configure dialog display

6. In *js/script.js*, modify the *.dialog()* method to provide these options and values:

   * *autoOpen: false*

   * *width: 500*

   * *modal: true*

7. Create a *submit button click* event handler.

8. Use the *event* object of this handler to prevent default form submission.

9. In this handler, select *offerdialog* and invoke the *open* option using the *.dialog()* method.

10. Your code should look like this:

```
$("#submit").on("click", function(event){
    event.preventDefault();
    $("#offerdialog").dialog("open");
});

$("#offerdialog").dialog({
                    autoOpen: false,
                    width: 500,
                    modal: true
                    });
```

11. Save your changes and browse *index.html*. Click the *submit button*. The *offerdialog* should open modally (with a grey, non-interactive background).

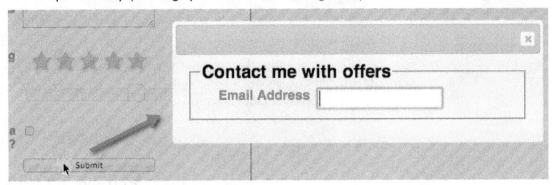

Configure dialog for conditional display and with buttons

12. In *js/script.js*, add a *buttons* option to the *.dialog()* method.

13. Assign buttons an *array* of inline *objects*, each with a *text* property, one assigned *Send offers* and the next *No thanks* as literal string values.

14. Your code should look like this:

```
$("#offerdialog").dialog({
                autoOpen: false,
                width: 500,
                modal: true,
                buttons: [{text:"Send offers"}, {text:"No thanks"}]
                });
```

15. In the *submit button click* handler, wrap the code opening *offerdialog* in a condition.

16. In this condition, select the *input* with the *name buy* and test whether it *.is() :checked*.

17. Your chode should look like this:

```
$("#submit").on("click", function(event){
      event.preventDefault();
      if($("input[name='buy']").is(":checked")) {
            $("#offerdialog").dialog("open");
      }
});
```

18. Save your changes and browse *index.html*. Open the browser console. Click the *submit button*. Nothing should happen. Check the *buy checkbox*, then click the *submit button*. The dialog should open, displaying two buttons *Send offers* and *No thanks*.

19. Click either *button*, and the console should display *Uncaught TypeError: Cannot call method 'apply' of undefined*.

Handle dialog button events

20. In *js/script.js*, modify the *.dialog()* method *buttons* option, to add *click* properties assigned an inline *function* receiving an *event* argument.

```
$("#offerdialog").dialog({
                        autoOpen: false,
                        width: 500,
                        modal: true,
                        buttons: [
                                {
                                        text:"Send offers",
                                        click: function(event) {

                                        }
                                },
                                {
                                        text:"No thanks",
                                        click: function(event) {

                                        }
                                }
                        ]
                });
```

21. In the *Send offers click* event handler, assign the value of the *input* named *email* to a local variable named *address*.

22. Select the *span* with *id offeremail* from the main form, and display *address* after the string *We'll send offers to* .

23. Use a *$(this)* reference to invoke the *.dialog()* method with the *close* option.

24. Your code should look like this:

```
...
modal: true,
buttons: [
        {
          text:"Send offers",
          click: function(event) {
            var address = $("input[name='email']").val();
            $("#offeremail").text("We'll send offers to " + address);
            $(this).dialog("close");
          }
        },
...
```

25. In the *No thanks click* event handler, assign an *empty string* to the *span* with *id offeremail*, then close *$(this)* dialog.

```
modal: true,
buttons: [
        { text: "Send offers", ... },
        {
          text:"No thanks",
          click: function(event) {
            $("#offeremail").text("");
            $(this).dialog("close");
          }
        }
      ]
});
```

26. Save your changes and browse *index.html*. Check the *buy checkbox*. Submit the form. Add an email address and click the *Send offers* button. The dialog should close, and the address appear with text at the bottom of the *offerwidgets div*.

27. Click the *submit button* a second time, the click *No thanks*. The dialog should close and the *offeremail div* should be cleared.

28. Close all project files.

Summary

In this unit you have learned:

- jQuery UI includes *Autocomplete, Button, Datepicker, Dialog, Slider,* and *Button* widgets

- Each is created by calling *$(selector).widget()* on an *input* or *div*

- Widget methods are invoked by passing the *method* name to the widget method itself

- Widgets are configured by passing objects assigned *option* values and *event* functions

- *Autocomplete* widgets use their *input* to look up *label* and *value* properties

- *Datepicker* widgets support i18n with pre-built localization objects

- *Datepicker* widgets can be significantly configured and interact with other *Datepickers*

- *Slider* widgets may select a single *value* or a range of *values*

- *Button* widgets create themed buttons and sets from a variety of underlying elements

- *Dialog* widgets create pop up display from a content *div* with configurable buttons

Review

1. You want users to select their airline departure and arrival dates. What widgets and events might you configure to usefully display this information?

2. If a *Slider* is presenting a price range for products to be searched, how do you determine the selected price range?

3. Why might you use *Button* widgets, instead of basic HTML *form* elements?

4. In a *Dialog* button, what does *$(this)* refer to?

5. Why might you provide different *label* and *value* properties in the data objects assigned as the source of an *Autocomplete* widget?

6. In a *form*, will data displayed in a *span* element be submitted along with the form?

Unit 10
Adding Validation and Effects to forms

Objectives

After completing this unit, you should understand:

- Implementing jQuery Validation in a project

- Assigning validation rules via HTML or JavaScript

- Customizing error message text, appearance, and display location

- Controlling validation timing and post-validation form submission

- Adding visual animation effects to page elements

Introducing jQuery Validation

jQuery provides straightforward, robust form data validation through the jQuery Validation plugin. While it is distributed separately from the jQuery site, it is developed and maintained by jQuery Project Board member Jörn Zaefferer.

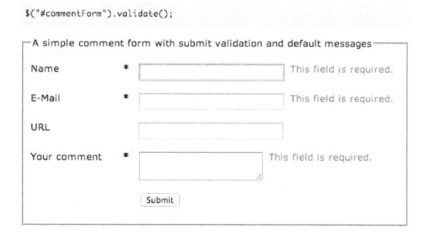

```
$("#commentForm").validate();
```

The jQuery Validation plugin is used by major sites including SoundCloud and Newsweek.

Knowing what can be tested

By assigning one or more validation classes to a form element, over a dozen distinct validation types can be assigned to a field, including:

- required fields

- minimum, maximum, and ranged value testing

- email address and URL format validity

- date, ISO date, decimal, digit, U.S. phone number, and credit card testing

- mime-type and file extension testing

Knowing when testing occurs

By default, validation is tested on all of these events. Unwanted testing can be suppressed.

- on form submit

- as each validated field loses focus

- on each key stroke in a validated field

Knowing where validation messages display

Default or custom validation messages can be displayed:

- individually in any selectable element

- or, collectively in a specified container, individually wrapped as specified

Implementing the jQuery Validation plugin

The jQuery Validation plugin is an optional library. The core implementation approach is to:

- add the jQuery Validation library to the page

```
<script type="text/javascript"
    src="js/jquery-validation-1.10.0/dist/jquery.validate.js"></script>
```

- assign specified class names to fields to be validated

```
<input name="meetingdate" class="required date"/>
```

- select the *form* element and invoke the *.validate()* method

```
$("#meetingform").validate();
```

- pass an options object to configure event and messaging

```
$("#meetingform").validate({
    messages: { meetingdate : "Valid date required" },
    errorClass: "error-display",
    onkeyup: false
});
```

Surveying the jQuery Validation API

required() required(if expression true) required(if function true)	remote(validation URL)
minlength(length) maxlength(length) rangelength(range)	min(value) max(value) range(range)
email() url()	date() dateISO()
number() digits()	creditCard() phoneUS()
equalTo()	accept(mimeType) extension(fileExtension)

Downloading and using the jQuery Validation plugin

The jQuery Validation plugin is linked at the jQuery site to this URL:

http://bassistance.de/jquery-plugins/jquery-plugin-validation/

It may also be pulled from GitHub at this URL:

https://github.com/jzaefferer/jquery-validation

It is added to the page like other jQuery libraries:

```
<script type="text/javascript"
        src="js/jquery-validation-1.10.0/dist/jquery.validate.js"></script>
<script type="text/javascript" src="js/script.js"></script>
```

Visually indicating field validation

jQuery Validation does not prescribe or implement any way to mark a field as required. A red asterisk symbol has become widely used to indicate required fields.

```
.error {
      color: #ff0000;
      font-weight: bold;
}
...
<form id="reviewform" action="">
  <fieldset>
    <legend>Classic Book Review</legend>
    <p>
      <label class="field" for="title">Book Title</label>
      <input name="title" class="required" /><span class="error">*</span>
    </p>
```

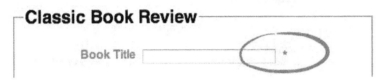

Assigning validation rules

Validation rules are specified by name, and can be assigned to *form* elements two ways:

- CSS validation class assigned to a field in HTML

  ```
  <input name="meetingdate" class="required date"/>
  ```

- Configuration options assigned as field *id rules* in jQuery

  ```
  <input name="meetingdate" />
  ...
  $("#meetingform").validate({
        rules: {
                meetingdate: {
                        required: true,
                        date: true
                }
        }
  });
  ```

Customizing error message appearance

jQuery provides default, unformatted error messages. By default, these messages are appended immediately following the validated field.

```
Classic Book Review
          Book Title [            ]This field is
    required.  *
```

A CSS class can be assigned to the *errorClass* property of an options object passed to the *.validate()* method, to customize error message display.

```css
.error-display {
      color: #ff0000;
      font-weight: bold;
}
...
$("#reviewform").validate({
      errorClass: "error-display"
});
```

```
Classic Book Review
          Book Title [            ]This field is
    required.  *
```

Note, recall that when configuring inline options, you are assigning properties to an inline JavaScript object, not writing JavaScript statements. If there is more than one option, separate each with a comma, though do not put a comma after the last. Do not end them with semi-colons.

Specifying error message placement

By default, error messages are appended immediately next to the validated element.

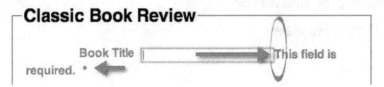

Message placement can be customized by assigning a *function* receiving *error* and *element* arguments to the *errorPlacement* option of the *.validate()* method.

error   error message as a string

element   form element to which the error applies

The *errorPlacement(error, element)* function can specify an alternate message placement.

```
$("#reviewform").validate({
     errorClass: "error-display",
     // append message following the error-display span (red asterisk)
     errorPlacement: function(error, element) {
          error.appendTo(element.siblings(".error-display"));
     }
});
```

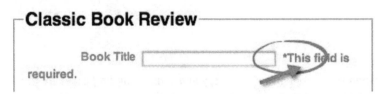

Grouping error message placement

jQuery Validation error messages can optionally be grouped in a container element containing a ul or ol element, specified using the *errorLabelContainer* option. Each message can be surrounded by the element specified using the *wrapper* option.

```
<div id="errormessages">
      <ul></ul>
</div>
<p>
      <label class="field" for="submit"> </label>
      <button id="submit">Submit</button>
</p>
...
$("#reviewform").validate({
      errorClass: "error-display",
      // append error messages to target list
      errorLabelContainer: "#errormessages",
      wrapper: "li"
});
```

- This field is required.
- This field is required.
- This field is required.

Submit

Customizing error message text

The default jQuery Validation messages can be changed by assigning alternate message values in the configuration object. Messages are assigned by element name to the messages property of the options object.

```
$("#reviewform").validate({
      errorClass: "error-display",
      // append error messages to target list
      errorLabelContainer: "#errormessages",
      wrapper: "li",
      // customize error messages
      messages: {
            title: "Title is required",
            reviewdate: "Review Date is required",
            comments: "Comments are required"
      }
});
```

- Title is required
- Review Date is required
- Comments are required

Submit

Exercise: Implement jQuery Validation

In this exercise you will configure a form for validation, including field requirement and content validation. You will control error message content, placement, and timing. And you will override default form submission behavior to occur through a defined function.

After completion, you should be able to:

- Implement jQuery Validation

- Configure required fields

- Control error message content, placement, and timing

- Validate fields for content

- Override form submission to occur following validation

Steps

Review project files

1. Open the following project and review its starting files.

   `/ftjq/10-validation`

2. Review *index.html* to notice within the form with *id reviewform*:

   - *offerdialog* from previous exercise removed

   - *email input* now displayed in *offerwidgets div*

   - *offeremail span* removed

```
<!-- Input for email user provides in dialog -->
<p>
    <!- <span id="offeremail"></span> ->
    <label class="field" for="offeraddress">Email Address</label>
    <input name="email" type="text" class="email" />
</p>
```

Implement the jQuery Validation library

3. Browse to one of these URLs:

   `https://github.com/jzaefferer/jquery-validation/downloads`

   `http://bassistance.de/jquery-plugins/jquery-plugin-validation/`

4. Download the jQuery *Validation* library.

   Note, jquery-validation-1.10.0.zip is provided in the project, if network access is not available

5. Extract the jQuery *Validation* archive to this location

   `/ftjq/9-validation/`**js**

6. Locate this file in the extracted archive:

   `/js/jquery-validation-1.10.0/dist/jquery.validate.js`

7. Add this library to the *index.html* page, <u>above</u> the project script *js/script.js*.

```
...
<script type="text/javascript" src="js/jquery-ui-i18n.min.js"></script>
<script type="text/javascript"
  src="js/jquery-validation-1.10.0/dist/jquery.validate.js"></script>
<script type="text/javascript" src="js/script.js"></script>
...
```

Visually identify required fields

8. In *css/style.css*, add a new *class error-display* with *color #ff0000* and *font-weight bold*.

```
.error-display {
        color: #ff0000;
        font-weight: bold;
}
```

9. In *index.html*, place an asterisk next to the *title*, *reviewdate*, and *comments input* elements, wrapped in a *span* element with *class required-icon*.

```
<p>
  <label class="field" for="title">Book Title</label>
  <input id="title" name="title" /><span class="error-display">*</span>
</p>
...
<p>
  <label class="field" for="reviewdate">Review Date</label>
  <input name="reviewdate"/><span class="error-display">*</span>
</p>
<p>
  <label class="field" for="comments">Comments</label>
  <textarea name="comments"></textarea><span class="error-display">*</span>
</p>
```

10. Save your changes and browse *index.html*. You should see red asterisks by the elements.

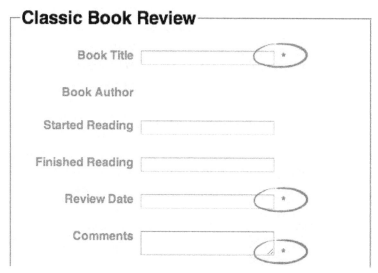

Identify fields to be validated by jQuery Validation

11. Add the *class required* to the *title*, *reviewdate*, and *comments input* elements.

```
<p>
  <label class="field" for="title">Book Title</label>
  <input id="title" name="title" class="required" />
      <span class="error-display">*</span>
</p>
...
<p>
  <label class="field" for="reviewdate">Review Date</label>
  <input name="reviewdate" class="required"/>
      <span class="error-display">*</span>
</p>
<p>
  <label class="field" for="comments">Comments</label>
  <textarea name="comments" class="required"></textarea>
      <span class="error-display">*</span>
</p>
```

Configure the reviewform for validation

12. In *js/script.js*, select and call the *.validate()* method on the *form* element *reviewform*.

```
$("#reviewform").validate();
```

13. Save your changes and browse *index.html*. <u>Submit</u> without filling in the required fields. You should see text messages directly following the fields, prior to the asterisks.

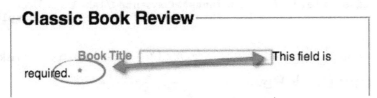

14. In *js/script.js*, modify the *.validate()* method to specify the *error-display* CSS class as the *errorClass* for this validation, using an inline options object.

```
$("#reviewform").validate({
      errorClass: "error-display"
});
```

Note, because you are assigning values to object properties - not writing a function as you commonly due inside curly braces - do <u>not</u> end this "statement" with a semi-colon. If there are multiple property assignments, you follow each but the last with a comma, following standard JavaScript object notation.

15. Save your changes and browse *index.html*. Submit the form without filling in the required fields. You should see formatted text messages, though they are still appended directly next to the validated fields.

Classic Book Review

Book Title   This field is
required.   *

Specify custom error messages

16. In *js/script.js*, modify the *.validate()* method to specify the custom message *Required* for the *title*, *reviewdate*, and *comments* fields. Carefully watch comma placement.

```
$("#reviewform").validate({
    errorClass: "error-display",
    messages: {
            title: "Required",
            reviewdate: "Required",
            comments: "Required"
    }
});
```

17. Save your changes and browse *index.html*. Submit the form. You should see the new error message displayed, though still before the asterisk.

Customize error message placement

18. In *js/script.js*, modify the *.validate()* method to add an *errorPlacement* property to the inline options object, and assign to it a *function* receiving *error* and *element* arguments.

19. In this *function*, append the *error* passed as an argument to the *sibling* of the *element* which dispatched the error, which has the *class error-display*.

20. Your code should look like this:

```
$("#reviewform").validate({
    errorClass: "error-display",
    messages: {
            title: "Required",
            reviewdate: "Required",
            comments: "Required"
    },
    errorPlacement: function(error, element) {
            error.appendTo(element.siblings(".error-display"));
    }
});
```

21. Save your changes and browse *index.html*. Submit the form. You should see the error message is now appended to the *error-display* span, rather than the field, so that now the asterisk appears before the message.

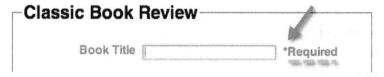

Note, you could use this approach to append the error message to virtually any element on the page which you select within the errorPlacement function.

Create summary error message display

22. In *index.html*, add a *div* with *id errormessages* above the *submit* button paragraph, then nested an empty *ul* element within this *div*.

```
<div id="errormessages">
        <ul></ul>
</div>
<p>
        <label class="field" for="submit"> </label>
        <button id="submit">Submit</button>
</p>
```

23. In *js/script.js*, in the *.validate()* method, <u>comment out</u> the *errorPlacement* function.

24. Add a property to the options object named *errorLabelContainer* and assign it the *id* of the *#errormessages div* as a string value, including the hash # symbol.

Note, if you neglect to use the hash symbol, error messages display, but as they did previously.

25. Add a property *wrapper* and assign it the string value *li*.

26. Your code should look like this:

```
$("#reviewform").validate({
        errorClass: "error-display",
        messages: {
                title: "Required",
                reviewdate: "Required",
                comments: "Required"
        },
        // errorPlacement: function(error, element) {
        //      error.appendTo(element.siblings(".error-display"));
        // },
        errorLabelContainer: "#errormessages",
        wrapper: "li"
});
```

27. Save your changes and browse *index.html*. Submit the form. You should see the error messages displayed in an unordered list above the submit button.

28. In *js/script.js*, modify the error message values to be understood away from the immediate context of their corresponding field.

```
$("#reviewform").validate({
        errorClass: "error-display",
        messages: {
                title: "Title is required",
                reviewdate: "Review Date is required",
                comments: "Comments are required"
        },
        ...
```

29. Save your changes and browse *index.html*. Submit the form. The error messages should now be understandable in a group.

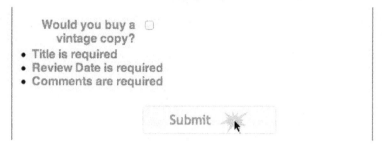

Note, you could place the container div and set wrapper elements however you choose (e.g., ordered list, add rows to a table, etc.)

30. Close all project files.

Controlling validation timing

By default, most types of jQuery Validation are applied at up to three points, depending on when there is sufficient information available to know if the field value is invalid. The following event options are true by default, and may be set false to suppress validation during the event for those validation types for which it would otherwise apply.

onkeyup   as the user completes each keystroke (example: email validation)

onfocusout   when focus leaves the field (example: date validation)

onsubmit   when the form submits (all validation, and required fields)

Detail on these events, and other .validate() options is available here:

http://docs.jquery.com/Plugins/Validation/validate

For example, by default email addresses are validated as the user types (onkeyup), as well as onfocusout and onsubmit. Set the onkeyup option to false to suppress validation while typing, while leaving validation as focus leaves each field, and when the form submits.

For example, to apply email validation to a field named email, that will only be enforced when the user tabs away from the field and/or submits the form:

```
$("#reviewform").validate({
    ...
    // apply email validation to input named email
    rules: {
        email: {
            email: true
        }
    },
    // suppress validation while typing
    onkeyup: false,
    ...
});
```

Controlling post-validation form submission

Implementing jQuery Validation suppresses normal form submission. Instead, a function specified by the submitHandler option is called. This function is passed a form argument, which can be used to control whether and how the form submits.

```
$("#reviewform").validate({
    errorClass: "error-display",
    messages: {
        title: "Title is required",
        reviewdate: "Review Date is required",
        comments: "Comments are required"
    },
    errorLabelContainer: "#errormessages",
    wrapper: "li",
    submitHandler: function(form){ alert("Submitted");}
});
```

Form submission is discussed further later in this unit.

Exercise: Assigning rules and controlling timing

In this exercise you will apply email validation by configuring the options object, optionally migrate all validation rules, and control email validation timing.

After completion, you should be able to:

- Assign validation rules using jQuery Validation options

- Control when validation rules are applied

Steps

Review project files

1. Open the following project and review its starting files.

   `/ftjq/10-timing`

2. The files are in the ending state from the previous exercise.

Configure email validation rule and timing

3. In *js/script.js*, configure the rules option for reviewform with a rule for the email input, with the email rule assigned as true.

```
$("#reviewform").validate({
    errorClass: "error-display",
    rules: {
        email: {
            email: true
        }
    },
    messages: {
        title: "Title is required",
        reviewdate: "Review Date is required",
        comments: "Comments are required"
    },
    errorLabelContainer: "#errormessages",
    wrapper: "li"
});
```

Note, recall that validation rules can be set either as CSS classes, or by the rules option, as shown.

4. (Optional) Migrate all validation from HTML into the *.validate()* method *rules* option.

5. Save your changes and browse *index.html*. Click the *buy* checkbox to open the *offerwidgets div*. Type in an email address. Notice the address is validated throughout the input. Red text is used for display, and the *errorLabelContainer* is used. When a valid address is entered the error message disappears and the text returns to normal.

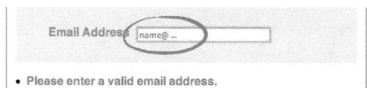

6. In *js/script.js*, modify the *.validate()* method to set the *onkeyup* property of the options object to *false* (it is true by default).

```
errorLabelContainer: "#errormessages",
wrapper: "li",
onkeyup: false
});
```

7. Save your changes and browse *index.html*. Click the *buy* checkbox to open the *offerwidgets div*. Type in an invalid address, then tab or click from the field. Notice validation is now happening when the field loses focus.

Note, recall that validation is true by default for onsubmit, onfocusout, onkeyup, and onclick for all validation. Any of these can be set to false to change validation behavior for the form.

Control form submission behavior

8. In *js/script.js*, modify the *.validate()* method to assign a *function* to the *submitHandler* property of the options object, and pass it a *form* argument.

9. In the function, display the word *Submitted* in a standard *alert()* box.

10. Your code should look like this:

```
errorLabelContainer: "#errormessages",
wrapper: "li",
onkeyup: false,
submitHandler: function(form){ alert("Submitted");}
});
```

11. Save your changes and browse *index.html*. Enter valid data for all fields, then click the *submit* button. The *alert* box should display.

12. Close all project files.

Controlling form submission

jQuery Validation suppresses form submission, in favor of calling a *submitHandler(form, event)* function. This approach opens multiple possibilities, including:

- AJAX submission to multiple URLs

- multiple format submission (HTML get/post and/or JSON via AJAX)

- pre-submit data manipulation not related to validation

Handling post-validation form submission

If a jQuery Validation *submitHandler* has been assigned, the form will not submit until the *submit()* method is called on the *form* object. If this method is not called, the form does not submit (which may be the intent in a fully client-side scenario).

```
$("#reviewform").validate({
    ...
    submitHandler: submitForm
});

function submitForm(form) {
    // log and modify validated data

    form.submit();
}
```

Ensuring jQuery UI Widget data capture

As seen, jQuery UI Widgets do not necessarily apply to *input* elements. Some may be applied to *div* or *span* elements, or may write data into such elements for display purposes.

However, only *input* data is submitted with a form. To account for this, Widget values can be written into corresponding *hidden input* elements. The default *value* of the widget should be assigned as the default *value* of the *hidden input*.

```
<!-- create display area and hidden data-holding input for ratingslider -->
<span id="rating"></span>
<input name="rating" type="hidden" value="5" />
<!-- create target element to be converted to a slider -->
<div id="ratingslider"></div>
...
$("#ratingslider").slider({
        // assign same default to hidden input as assigned to slider
        animate: "slow", value: 5, min: 1, max: 7, step: 1,
        // display current value as stars in rating span
        slide: function(event, ui) {
                showStars($("#rating"), ui.value);
                $("input[name='rating']").val(ui.value);
        }
});
```

Exercise: Capture selected and default data for jQuery UI widgets

In this exercise you will add hidden form fields to capture the values selected by the user for the jQuery UI widgets, to ensure all form elements are included in the submitted data.

After completion, you should be able to:

- Assign relevant input elements to capture data assigned through jQuery UI widgets

- Submit validated form data

Steps

Review project files

1. Open the following project and review its starting files.

    `/ftjq/10-submission`

2. The *index.html* and *js/script.js* files match the end state of the previous exercise.

3. The file *data/review.php* has been added to the project.

Manage form submission

4. In *js/script.js*, write a *function submitHandler* which receives *form* and *event* arguments.

5. Modify the options of the *$("#reviewForm").validate()* method to call the *submitHandler(form, event)* function as the submit handler for this form.

6. In the *submitHandler(form, event)* function, prevent form submission.

7. Create a jQuery object using the *form* argument, call its *.serialize()* method, and *.log()* the result. Also log the *event* argument.

8. Your code should look like this:

```
$("#reviewform").validate({
    errorClass: "error-display",
    messages: {
        title: "Title is required",
        reviewdate: "Review Date is required",
        comments: "Comments are required"
    },
    errorLabelContainer: "#errormessages",
    wrapper: "li",
    onkeyup: false,
    submitHandler: submitHandler
});

function submitHandler(form, event) {
    console.log($(form).serialize());
    console.log(event);
    form.submit();
}
```

9. Save your changes and browse *index.html*. Open the browser JavaScript console. Assign a value for every field on the form, whether required or not, and submit the form.

10. In the serialized output, notice which form fields are missing:

   • Author name

   • Rating

   • Low and high buy offers

Configure data capture from UI Autocomplete widget

11. In *index.html*, to avoid naming conflict, remove the *name* attribute from the *span* which displays the author value

12. Add a *hidden input* field with the *name author*.

13. Your code should look like this:

```
<p>
    <label class="field" for="author">Book Author</label>
    <span id="author"> </span>
    <input name="author" type="hidden" />
</p>
```

14. In *js/script.js*, locate the inline *function* handling *select* events from the *$("#title").autocomplete()* method.

15. In this *function*, assign the *ui.item.author* as the *.val()* of the new *hidden input*.

16. Your code should look like this:

```
$("#title").autocomplete({
        // assign books array as the autocomplete source
        source: books,
        // handle select events by displaying author data
        select: function(event, ui){
            $("#author").text(ui.item.author);
            $("input[name='author']").val(ui.item.author);
        }
    });
```

17. Save your changes and browse *index.html*. Complete all required files, and submit the form. You should see there is now an *author* parameter populated by the author of the selected book.

```
title=Ulysse s&author=James+Joyce& tartdate=01%2F21%2F2013&finishdate=
01%2F28%2F2013&reviewdate=01%2F28%2F2013&comments=A+might+tome.&ratin
g=4&buy=on&condition=Fine&offerlow=11&email=name%40address.com
                                                           script.js:23
```

Configure data capture from UI Slider widgets

18. In *index.html*, add a *hidden input* field named *rating* to capture this value from the *ratingslider* UI widget. Assign this element a *value* of *5* to correspond to the default rating assigned to this widget in *js/script.js*.

```html
<p>
    <label class="field" for="rating">Rating</label>
    <span id="rating"></span>
    <input name="rating" type="hidden" value="5" />
    <div id="ratingslider"></div>
</p>
```

19. In *js/script.js*, modify the inline *function* handling *slide* events dispatched by the *ratingslider* UI Widget to assign the *ui.value* property to the new *input* field.

```javascript
$("#ratingslider").slider({
        animate: "slow",
        value: defaultRating,
        min: 1,
        max: 7,
        step: 1,
        slide: function(event, ui) {
                showStars($("#rating"), ui.value);
                $("input[name='rating']").val(ui.value);
        }
});
```

20. Save your changes and browse *index.html*. Complete all required fields, move the slider to select a *rating* value, and submit the form. You should now see a *rating* parameter with the selected rating value.

```
title Ul      s&author=James+Joyce&startdate=01%2F20%2F2013&finishdate:
&rating=6&c ndition=on&email=
▶ jQuery.Event {originalEvent: Event, type: "submit", isDefaultPreven
  jQuery19003235841956920922: true...}

>
```

21. In *index.html*, add *hidden input* fields named *offerlow* and *offerhigh* to capture these values from the *offerslider* UI widget. Assign these elements the values *10* and *150* to correspond to the default *values* assigned to this widget in *js/script.js*.

```
<p>
    <label class="field" for="offer">What would you offer?</label>
    <span id="offer"></span>
    <input name="offerlow" type="hidden" value="10" />
    <input name="offerhigh" type="hidden" value="150" />
    <div id="offerslider"></div>
</p>
```

22. In *js/script.js*, modify the *function* handling *slide* events dispatched by the *offerslide* UI widget to assign the *ui.values[0]* (low) and *ui.values[1]* (high) to their new corresponding *hidden input* fields.

```
$("#offerslider").slider({
    range: true,
    min: 1,
    max: 250,
    values: [10, 150],
    step: 1,
    slide: function(event, ui) {
        $("#offer").text("$" + ui.values[0] + " - " + "$" + ui.values[1]);
        $("input[name='offerlow']").val(ui.values[0]);
        $("input[name='offerhigh']").val(ui.values[1]);
    }
});
```

23. Save your changes and browse *index.html*. Complete all required fields, check the *Buy* box, and modify the *Offer* slider. Submit the form. You should see the new *offerlow* and *offerhigh* parameters in the serialized form output.

Capturing output from a UI buttonset widget

24. In the console output from the previous step, notice the value displayed for the *condition* buttonset: *on*.

Fast Track to jQuery

25. In *index.html,* modify each of the three *condition radio* elements to include a *value* attribute, with a Good, Fine, or Mint value corresponding to the related label element.

```
<p>
  <label class="field" for="condition">Book condition</label>
  <div id="conditionbuttonset">
    <input id="condition1" type="radio" name="condition" value="Good" />
      <label for="condition1">Good</label>
    <input id="condition2" type="radio" name="condition" value="Fine" />
      <label for="condition2">Fine</label>
    <input id="condition3" type="radio" name="condition" value="Mint"
      checked="checked" />
      <label for="condition3">Mint</label>
  </div>
</p>
```

26. Save your changes and browse *index.html.* Complete all required fields. Check the *Buy* button, and select a *Condition* from the *condition* buttonset. Submit the form. You should now see the selected value for the *condition* parameter.

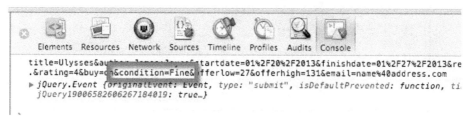

Submit the validated form

27. In *index.html,* modify *reviewform* to add an *action* attribute submitting to *data/review.php.*

```
<form id="reviewform" action="data/review.php">
      <fieldset>
            <legend>Classic Book Review</legend>
```

28. In *js/script.js,* modify the *submitHandler(form, event)* function to comment out the *event.preventDefault()* method invocation, and add an *event.submit()* method invocation.

```
function submitHandler(form, event ) {
      // event.preventDefault();
      console.log($(form).serialize());
      console.log(event);
      event.submit();
}
```

29. Save your changes and browse *index.html.* Complete the form, assigning a value to every field. Submit the form. You should see all fields display their values from the script.

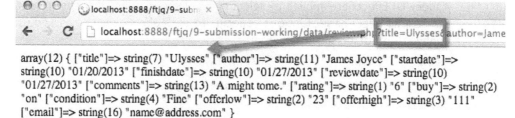

array(12) { ["title"]=> string(7) "Ulysses" ["author"]=> string(11) "James Joyce" ["startdate"]=> string(10) "01/20/2013" ["finishdate"]=> string(10) "01/27/2013" ["reviewdate"]=> string(10) "01/27/2013" ["comments"]=> string(13) "A might tome." ["rating"]=> string(1) "6" ["buy"]=> string(2) "on" ["condition"]=> string(4) "Fine" ["offerlow"]=> string(2) "23" ["offerhigh"]=> string(3) "111" ["email"]=> string(16) "name@address.com" }

30. Close all project files.

Augmenting user feedback with jQuery UI Effects

Introducing jQuery UI Effects

jQuery UI Effects are pre-built animations which can be applied to visual elements. Selective use of animation can both enhance the user experience and add information. Overuse is annoying.

For example, a login form could shake horizontally or vertically to indicate whether authentication succeeded.

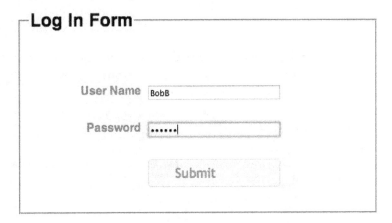

Surveying the available effects

The following jQuery UI Effects are available.

Effects	blind	bounce	clip	drop	explode
	fade	fold	highlight	puff	pulsate
	scale	shake	size	slide	transfer

Details of each can be found here:

http://API.jQueryUI.com/1.9/category/Effects/

Implementing a jQuery UI Effect

jQuery UI Effects are applied by selecting an element, calling the *.effect()* method, and passing the desired effect name. Options - specific to each effect - may be passed using an inline configuration objects.

```
<span id="pulse">How's my pulse?</span>
...
$("#pulse").effect("pulsate", {times: 7});
```

Handling form responses without a page reload

Sending data via AJAX without form submission

As review, submitting a form reloads the page. The *$.ajax()* method can send data and update the page without this page reload.

```html
<form id="loginform" action="">
  <span id="result"></span>
  <input id="username" />
  <input id="password" type="password" />
  <button id="submit">Submit</button>
</form>
...
```

```javascript
$("#submit").on("click", function(event){
  event.preventDefault();

  var username = $("#username").val();
  var password = $("#password").val();

  $.ajax({
    url: "data/login.php",
    type: "GET",
    contentType: "application/json",
    data: {
      username: username,
      password: password
    },
    success: loginHandler,
    error: errorHandler
  });

});
```

Handling JSON responses

A remote script can provide a data-only response by outputting JSON as the result of a page request. This string *result* is passed as an argument to the *$.ajax()* success handler. It can then be parsed from string JSON into JavaScript data, using the *$.parseJSON(value)* method.

The results can then be displayed, and effects applied to provide an engaging user experience.

```javascript
function loginHandler(result) {
  var user = $.parseJSON(result);
  if (user.login === "valid") {
    // display user name as authenticated
    $("#result").text(user.firstName + " " + user.lastName + " authenticated");
    $("#loginform").effect("bounce");
    $("#result").effect("pulsate", {times: 7});
  } else {
    $("#loginform").effect("shake");
  }
}
```

Exercise: Using Effects for non-reloading form feedback

In this exercise you will submit login form data and receive a JSON response. You will parse the result to determine if the login succeeded, and provide appropriate visual effects.

After completion, you should be able to:

- Submit form data and parse the results as JSON

- Add jQuery UI Effects to enhance the user experience

Steps

Review project files

1. Open the following project and review its starting files.
   `/ftjq/10-effects`

2. Open *index.html* to review the form with *id loginform*

   - *input* elements with *id username* and *password*

   - *submit button* with *id submit*

   - *span* with *id result*

3. Browse *index.html*.

4. Open *js/script.js* to review its pre-built code:

   - *submit button* configured for jQuery UI *Button* display

   - *click* event handler for *submit button*

   - *loginHandler* and *errorHandler* functions

Configure initial form display effect

5. In *js/script.js*, add a *slide effect* to *loginform*, which runs as the page initially loads.

```
$(document).ready(function(){

    $("#loginform").effect("slide");
```

6. Save your changes and browse *index.html*. The form should slide in from left to right.

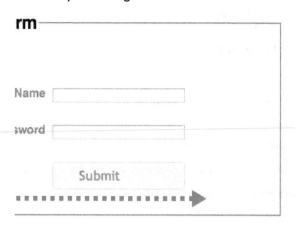

7. In *js/script.js*, modify the *slide* effect by adding an inline options object after the effect name. Set the *direction* property to *up*.

```
$("#loginform").effect("slide", {direction: "up"});
```

8. Browse *index.html*. The form should slide <u>from</u> (not to) the specified direction.

Gather and submit form data

9. In *js/script.js*, in the *click* event handler for the *submit button*, capture the values from the *username* and *password* fields, and assign them to like-named variables.

10. Clear these two fields after capturing their data by assigning them an empty string.

11. Your code should look like this:

```
$("#submit").on("click", function(event){
        event.preventDefault();

        var username = $("#username").val();
        $("#username").val("");

        var password = $("#password").val();
        $("#password").val("");
        ...
```

12. Using the *$.ajax()* method, submit the *username* and *password* to *data/login.php* as a *GET type* request.

13. Configure the submission to expect JSON as the resulting *contentType*.

14. Call *loginHandler* if the request is a *success* and *errorHandler* if there is an *error*.

15. In *loginHandler*, log the *result* argument returned by the request.

16. Your code should look like this:

```
$("#submit").on("click", function(event){
        event.preventDefault();

        var username = $("#username").val();
        $("#username").val("");

        var password = $("#password").val();
        $("#password").val("");

        $.ajax({
                url: "data/login.php",
                type: "GET",
                contentType: "application/json",
                data: {
                        username: username,
                        password:password
                },
                success: loginHandler,
                error: errorHandler
        });

});

function loginHandler(result) {
        console.log(result);
}
function errorHandler(result) {
        console.log(result)
}
```

17. Save your changes and browse *index.html*. Open the JavaScript console. Log in with username *TinaT* (not case sensitive) and password *password*. You should see a valid login object displayed in the console.

18. Log in with username *Fred* and password *Foo*. You should see an invalid login object displayed in the console.

19. (Optional) Open and review *data/login.php* to see how the server data is generated.

Note, data/login.php is written for demonstration purposes. Actual user authentication would happen via HTTPS, and involve an encrypted user data storage mechanism, all of which are outside the scope of this jQuery training content.

Engage the user with visual effects

20. In *js/script.js*, if the AJAX request is successful, parse the *result* argument, which is the string returned by the server, as JSON, assigning the result to a variable named *user*.

```
function loginHandler(result) {
      console.log(result);
      var user = $.parseJSON(result);

}
```

21. Using the *user.login* property, test whether *user.login* has the value *valid* or *invalid*.

22. If the login is *invalid*, shake the form.

```
function loginHandler(result) {
      console.log(result);
      var user = $.parseJSON(result);
      if (user.login === "valid") {

      } else {
            $("#loginform").effect("shake");
      }
}
```

23. Save your changes and browse *index.html*. Attempt to log in with user name *Fred* and password *Foo*. The form should shake in respond to the invalid login.

24. Regardless of whether the login is valid or invalid - *above the condition* - clear the *result span* by assigning an empty string as its *.text()*.

25. If the login is *valid*, display the *user.firstName* and *user.lastName* in the *result span* and indicate the user is authenticated.

26. If the login is *valid*, *pulsate* the *result span* 7 times and *bounce* the *loginform* itself.

27. Your code should look like this:

```
function loginHandler(result) {
  console.log(result);
  var user = $.parseJSON(result);
  $("#result").text("");
  if (user.login === "valid") {
    $("#result").text(user.firstName + " " + user.lastName + " authenticated");
    $("#loginform").effect("bounce");
    $("#result").effect("pulsate", {times: 7});
  } else {
    $("#loginform").effect("shake");
  }
}
```

28. Save your changes and browse *index.html*. Log in with user name *TinaT* and password *password*. You should see the name *Tina Tourquoise* pulsate and appear on the form, which bounces up and down to indicate success.

29. Close all project files.

Summary

In this unit you have learned:

- jQuery Validation is a distinct library

- Fields can be required, and tested for min, max, range, and a variety of formats

- Validation rules can be applied in HTML or JavaScript

- Error messages can be visually and textually customized

- Error messages can be individual placed, or summarily grouped

- Validation timing can be controlled

- When using validation, form submission can be routed through a handler function

- If handled, the form only submits if *form.submit()* or *event.submit()* are called

- Only *input* values submit with a form, so Widget values may need to be written to hidden input *elements*

- Data captured by a form can be sent, and JSON responses handled, without submitting the form at all

- Visual effects can be easily applied to enhance the user experience

Review

1. You want individual validation errors on a password field to be logged to a remote server as they occur. How could you approach doing this?

2. You want to restrict file uploads by file extension and mime-type. Can this be done using jQuery Validation?

3. You need to specify how many buttons appear in a jQuery UI Button set based on a value selected somewhere else on the form, but without submitting the form. The number of buttons, and their labels, can be queried live from a remote script. How could you create this effect?

4. Your designer wants a series of images to slide on from one side of the page, then slide off the other side. How would you approach doing this?

5. Your boss wants you to build a highly interactive, JavaScript intensive site without jQuery. What do you do?

Appendix A
Setup Guide

Introducing the system requirements

To use this training material you will need:

- a text editor
- a modern web browser with a JavaScript console
- a local web server running the PHP application server
- the course files archive provided with these training materials

Any system configuration meeting these requirements will work for this training.

These materials were developed using these tools:

- Google Chrome v.24, Firefox v.18, and Safari v.6
- Sublime Text 2
- MAMP: Mac + Apache + MySQL + PHP
  http://www.mamp.info

Choosing and installing development tools

Choosing a text editor

Because HTML, CSS, and JavaScript files are plain text, literally any text editor may be used for this course. That being said, some choices are better than others.

You may wish to review and consider one of these:

Sublime Text 2
http://www.sublimetext.com/2

Jetbrains WebStorm
http://www.jetbrains.com/webstorm/

Notepad++
http://notepad-plus-plus.org/

TextMate
http://macromates.com/

Choosing a web browser

The real answer for a web developer is that there is no "one" answer. You need to support them all, and this sometimes painful reality is one reason why you'll enjoy using jQuery.

That being said, many developers choose to rely on either *Mozilla Firefox* with *Firebug* installed, for testing and debugging, or Google *Chrome*, with its built-in developer tools, for the core development process; leaving the other browsers for later pre-launch testing.

Get Google Chrome

http://www.google.com/chrome

Get Mozilla Firefox and Firebug

http://www.mozilla.org/

http://www.getfirebug.com

Get Opera

http://www.opera.com/download

Get Safari

http://www.apple.com/safari

Get Internet Explorer 9

http://windows.microsoft.com/en-US/internet-explorer/download-ie

Checking browser support and performance

Detailed information on browser support for various aspects of HTML, CSS, and JavaScript can be found here:

http://caniuse.com/

Detailed information on the performance of various JavaScript code operations on various browsers can be found here:

http://jsperf.com

Locating the JavaScript console and developer tools

Chrome
Tools > JavaScript Console
Tools > Developer Tools

Firefox
Tools > Web Developer > Web Console
Tools > Web Developer > Firebug (additional plugin)

Safari (Preferences > Advanced > Show Develop menu in menu bar)
Develop > Show Error Console

Internet Explorer 9
F12 > Console

Installing a web server and PHP

A local web server is required for this course, because jQuery loads remote data via HTTP.

*__Warning__: if you are working on an exercise which involves loading external data, **you __must__ request the page using http:// and __not__ file:// or jQuery will fail** to load the external data or request the remote script.*

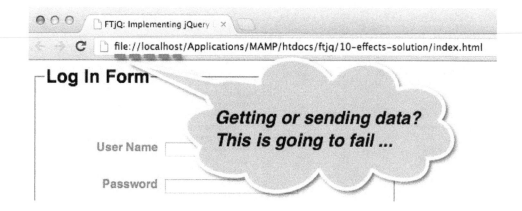

A PHP application server installation is required for this course, because some exercises rely on sending and receiving data from a remote script. **No PHP knowledge is required**. You may safely ignore all .php script files in this course, and simply let them complete their function.

You may already have a local web server and PHP installed. If so, and you are familiar with them, then use them. If so, you will need to remember to use your port address rather than the port address you see in the training material.

If you do not already have Apache and PHP installed, it is very easy to install one of these pre-built, open source configurations.

Mac

For Mac, it is easy to download and use MAMP.

MAMP

http://www.mamp.info

Windows

For Windows, it is easy to download and use WampServer.

WampServer

http://www.wampserver.com

Installing the course files

Use an archive utility to extract this file to the web root folder of your web server. This archive will create a /ftjq folder, with a series of sub-folders including HTML, CSS, JavaScript, and jQuery libraries used for each course exercise.

```
ftjq-coursefiles-[date].zip
```

For example, if you are using the MAMP server, your file system would look like this:

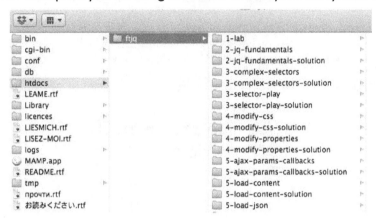

Testing the course files

1. Launch your PHP application server

2. Browse this URL (adding your PHP server's correct port number)

   `http://localhost:[port]/ftjq/10-effects-solution/index.html`

3. Submit the form with these values:

   • *Username: BobB*

   • *Password: password*

4. You should see the following: